5 September 1991

CW01671613

STARTING
EMBROIDERY

Jenny Bullen

B. T. Batsford Ltd, London

© Jenny Bullen 1989
First published in 1989

All rights reserved. No part of this publication may be reproduced, in any form or by any means, without permission from the Publisher.

ISBN 0 8521 9792 6

Set in Monotype Palatino
Typeset by Latimer Trend & Company Ltd
and printed in Great Britain by
Courier International, Tiptree, Essex
for the Publishers
B. T. Batsford Ltd
4 Fitzhardinge Street
London W1H 0AH

Photographs by Jim Pascoe
Illustrations by Clive Yeomans

A CIP record for this book is available from the British Library.

Contents

Introduction

In writing this book I have considered primarily the needs of embroiderers whose previous experience has been working with kits or designs from charts (in other words, other people's ideas!) and who are now ready to move on a little further and begin to think for themselves.

The obvious course for these people is to join an embroidery class, and I hope that they will do just that. There are many local authority run classes in creative embroidery up and down the country. In addition, short residential courses are often available—for a weekend or a few days. However, it is not always possible to join a class or to find the money or time to get away for a few days. I hope that my book will be of some use to people who find themselves in just that situation.

It is not, I would emphasise, a 'complete book of embroidery'. I have chosen six techniques which I feel that a beginner might quite easily cope with and enjoy working with, and, above all, be able to purchase the appropriate equipment quite easily and at fairly low cost. I have omitted some very popular types of embroidery, such as patchwork and machine embroidery, as these require books to themselves. I have also included a chapter on materials and threads, and information on dressing embroidery frames, transferring designs etc. The last chapter is about finishing off and making simple tassels and cords.

I hope, however, that through the subjects covered here I have given some ideas and starting points. Do buy a sketch book and use it. Make lots of samplers and experimental pieces, and don't throw away the pieces you hate. Keep them, and in a few months you will find that they are not so bad after all. Visit as many museums, art galleries and exhibitions as possible. Go to classes whenever possible. Talk to people (embroiderers and those involved in other crafts); it is very difficult to work in isolation. Above all, have the courage of your convictions–buy some calico and a few threads and just begin!

One

Materials and equipment

Some basic embroidery equipment is necessary. However, this need not all be purchased at once; the cost of these items is relatively low and, if well cared for, they will last for a very long time.

A good stitch dictionary is essential. It should have a good, explanatory text and clear diagrams. Keep a scrapbook of magazine and newspaper cuttings, and photographs of anything of interest, for use as source material for future embroideries.

Needles

A variety of different needles will be needed and suggestions for appropriate ones are given with each chapter. Among those suggested are various sizes of crewel and tapestry needles. Crewel needles have sharp points and long, narrow eyes, and are suitable for a wide range of embroidery threads. Tapestry needles have blunt ends and are used for counted thread embroidery. Large-eyed needles for taking thicker threads, such as chenille or knitter's needles, are useful. Beading needles are very long and slender, and useful when working with beads and sequins.

You will also need fine, rustless pins and a thimble. A stiletto is useful for piercing holes in background fabrics when working with very thick threads. A pair of dressmaking scissors and a small pair of embroidery scissors with fine sharp points are essential. Hide them away from the rest of the family, and use them *only* for cutting fabrics and threads.

Frames

Although it is not absolutely essential to work embroidery in a frame, it does help to keep the fabric taut and in shape, and allows the use of both hands whilst working.

A medium sized wooden hoop (tambour frame) is essential for experiments and small pieces of work. Before using, bind the inner ring with tape, which helps to give a firmer grip and avoids damaging the fabric. After binding, oversew the tape so that it will not move or become unravelled once the fabric is placed in the ring.

To use a tambour frame, lay the fabric between the two rings and pull taut by tightening the screw on the outer ring. Be careful, however, not to distort the weave of the fabric.

For working larger pieces of embroidery you will need to purchase a square frame. It is possible to buy slate frames from embroidery suppliers, but these tend to be rather expensive. Cheaper alternatives are artist's stretchers, or a simple homemade frame. When making a frame, choose a fairly soft wood so that drawing pins can be pushed easily into the edges. Alternatively, strips of double sided adhesive tape can be stuck around the edge and the fabric carefully smoothed over it.

Threads

There is a great abundance of varieties of embroidery threads on the market today, which can be quite bewildering to a beginner.

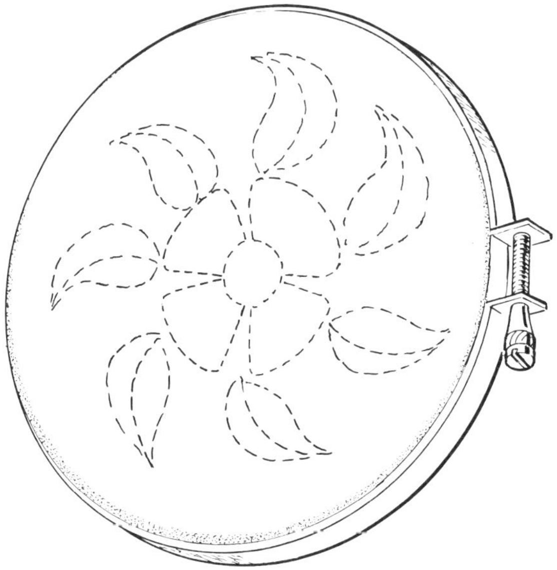

Fig. 1. Ring or tambour hoop. The fabric should be pulled as taut as possible without distorting the weave

Fig. 2. Slate frame. To dress a slate or square frame:
(a) Mark the centres of the two strips of webbing and the centres of the fabric to be embroidered
(b) Turn under the raw edges of the fabric and pin to the webbing, matching the centres
(c) Working from the centre outwards, oversew the fabric in place, using a strong thread
(d) Slot the side bars in place and pull the frame so that the fabric is as taut as possible without tearing the fabric
(e) Place the pegs in the appropriate holes
(f) Using a very strong thread or fine string, lace the fabric to the slats

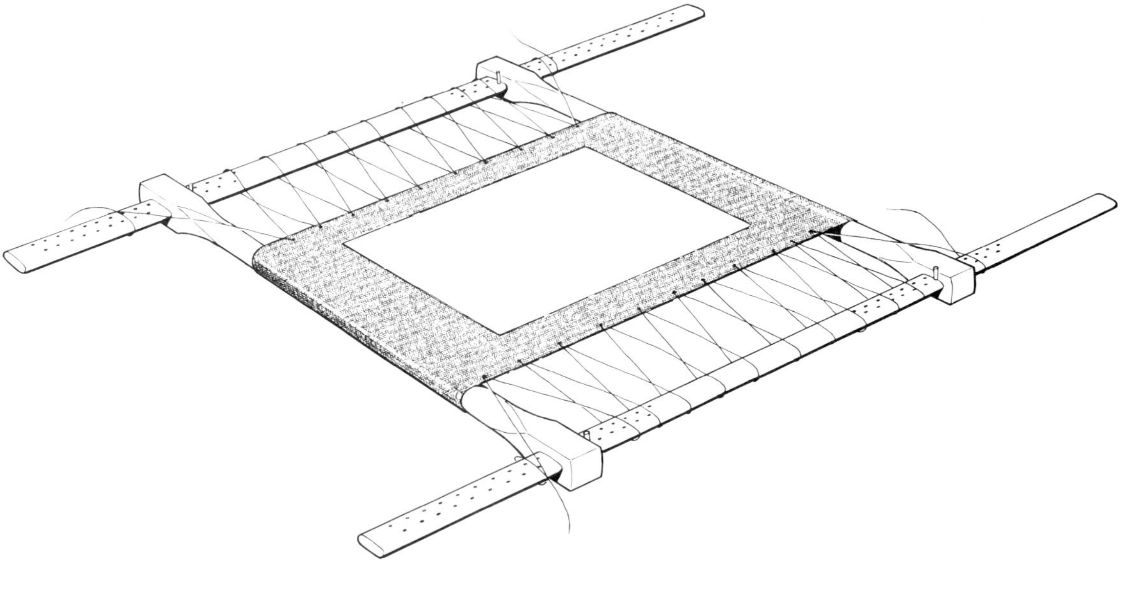

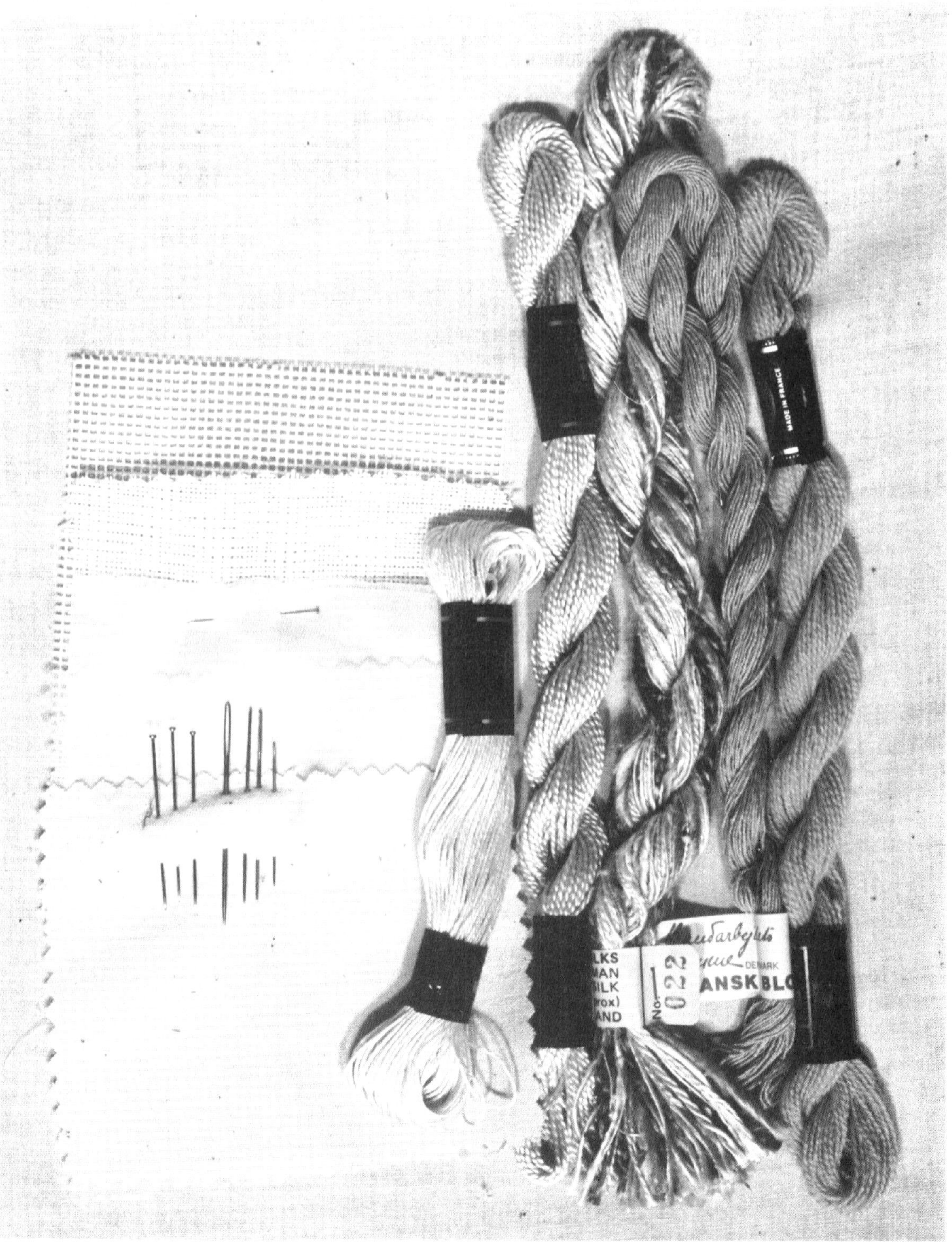

Fig. 3. A very small selection of some of the threads and fabrics available to the embroiderer today. The threads are coton à broder, cotton perlé, textured silks, flower thread and tapestry wool. The fabrics are canvas, evenweave linen, fine silk and calico

Stranded embroidery threads, coton à broder, perlés of different weights and other standard threads can all be purchased at specialist shops. There, you will also find other interesting threads to use, such as lurex, fine ribbons, crewel wools, etc. Pure silk threads are available in a wide range of beautiful colours at some embroidery shops. Threads can be stored in clear plastic sweet jars, which confectioners usually throw away once they are empty.

Fabrics

As with threads, the choice of fabrics is overwhelming. They can, however, be purchased in short lengths and pieces shared among friends. A good quality medium-weight unbleached calico is excellent value. It is reasonably inexpensive and can be used for background fabrics, as well as for experimental pieces. Dress-weight polyester cotton is also useful. It has a slight sheen (useful when quilting) and takes fabric paints well. Both of these can be obtained easily from fabric departments of local stores. Look out, also, for remnants of furnishing fabrics. Pure silk is a beautiful, luxurious fabric and will, in its natural state, take dyes well. However, it is more expensive, and a little more difficult to handle, than most cottons.

For counted thread work you will need even weave fabric and canvas, which can be obtained from specialist shops, where you will also find unusual fabrics, such as coloured organzas, nets, lurex, suedes and leathers. These are usually sold in small quantities, which is especially suitable for the embroiderer who does not require large quantities.

Drawing and design equipment

If you wish to start to create your own designs you will need some basic drawing equipment.

The most important item is a sketchbook in which to record sketches, notes, photographs etc. This need not be an expensive, bound book; any sketchbook will do as long as it has reasonable quality cartridge paper. You will also need:

a good steel ruler, which can also be used for cutting mounts

a good quality craft knife

graphite pencils, ranging from medium (HB) to very soft (6B) and some coloured pencils (water-soluble crayons are quite useful)

paints—a small box of water-colours or a few tubes of gouache will be enough (student quality is quite adequate)

a number of brushes of differing sizes

good quality cartridge paper.

It is worth investigating children's arts and crafts suppliers, who usually have a good range of coloured paper, tissue paper, crayons and pencils and other items. These are usually quite cheap and can be great fun to experiment with.

Dyes and fabric paints

If you cannot find the exact colour of fabric and threads that you require, try dyeing some yourself. The easiest dyes to use are the fibre-reactive cold water dyes, which can easily be obtained in small quantities in local stores. These are suitable for dyeing natural fibres.

Collect a variety of fabrics and threads which can all be dyed together. Natural and pale colours will take the dye best, but it is worth experimenting with other colours and printed fabrics as well. The fabrics should all be washed beforehand to remove any dressing. Instructions are provided with the dye and should be followed carefully. One dye manufacturer has now produced a range of 'natural' dyes suitable for use in an automatic washing machine. This dye is much more expensive, but works well and does not stain the machine.

Fabric paints have appeared on the market in the last few years. These can be sprayed, sponged or painted on the fabric before the embroidery is worked. The most useful are the 'all purpose' paints. These are painted directly on to the fabric and are therefore suitable for both synthetics and

Fig. 4. A sample worked from studies of old, crumbling walls. Fabric paints have been sponged onto the calico background, and free stitchery, mainly couching and cretan stitch, worked on top (Barbara Mellor)

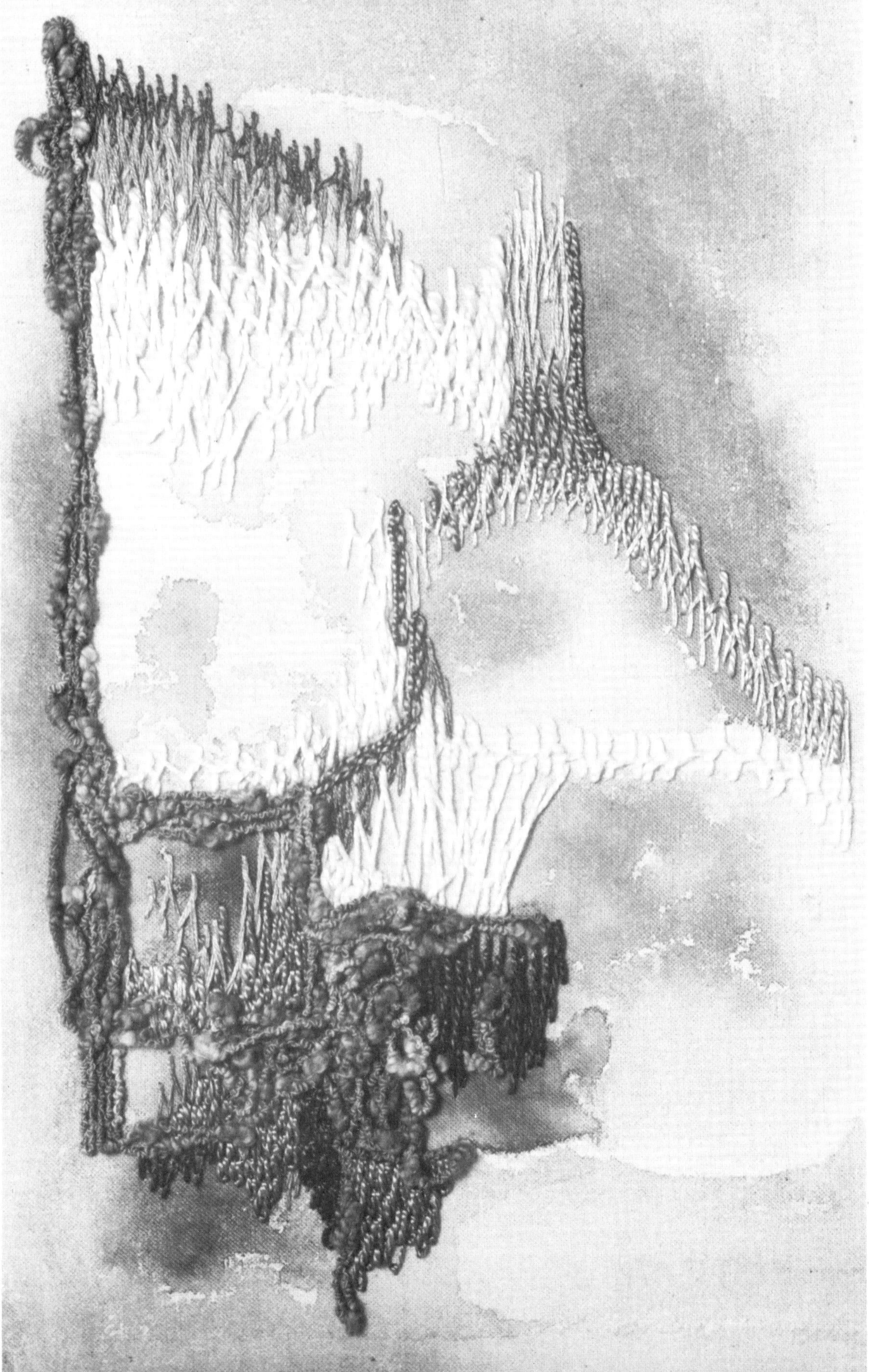

natural fibres. They can be mixed together to obtain a wide variety of colours. When dry, they are made colour-fast by pressing with a hot iron on the reverse side of the fabric for two or three minutes.

Silk paints are, obviously, created especially for silk fabrics and are usually 'fixed' by immersion in a chemical bath or by steaming. One or two manufacturers have produced silk paints that can be fixed by ironing.

Transfer paints are first painted on paper and then transferred by placing the paper face down on the fabric and pressing with a hot iron. These are meant for use on man-made fibres, but work very well on polyester cotton. Transfer paints need to be experimented with before use, as the colour seen on the paper is not always the same when transferred to fabric; they can be very garish. Remember, too, that when working your design on the paper, you need to reverse the image. However, all the techniques used with direct fabric paints can be used successfully with jetransfer paints, working first on paper. Transfer paints are especially useful if a hard outline is required, as direct paints tend to bleed into the background. Dye pens, for drawing directly onto

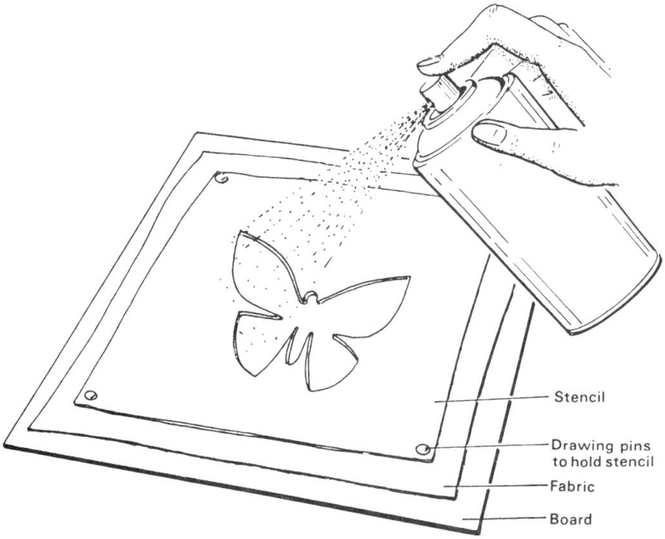

Fig. 5. Stencils may be cut from thin card or waxed stencil paper. When cutting stencils, make sure that the surrounding card is large enough to cover the fabric. If not, when using a diffuser or aerosol the exposed fabric is likely to be marked

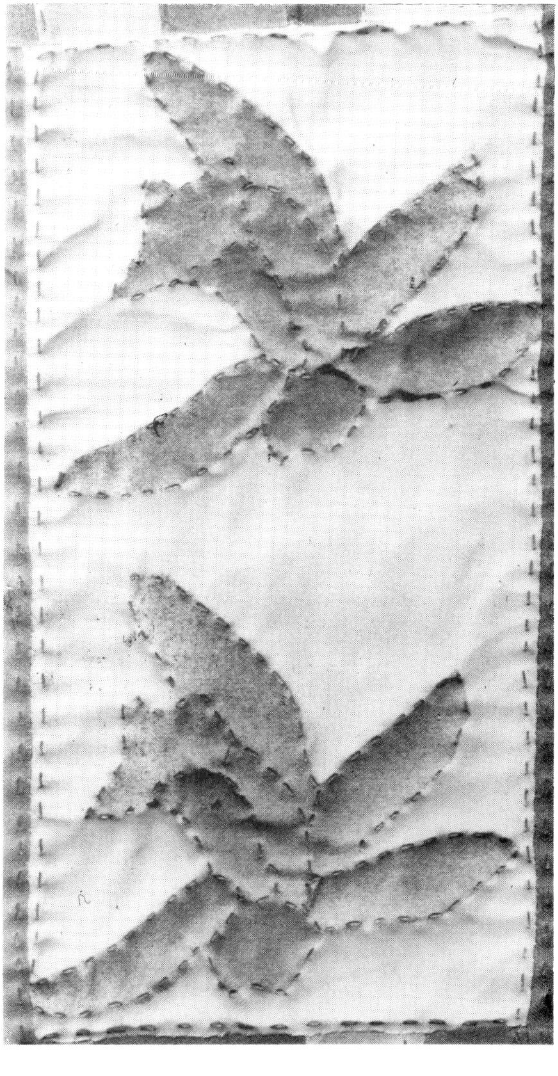

Fig. 6. Car spray paint was sprayed through a stencil on to silk fabric to produce the flowers, which are part of a larger hanging. It was then hand quilted (Jenny Bullen)

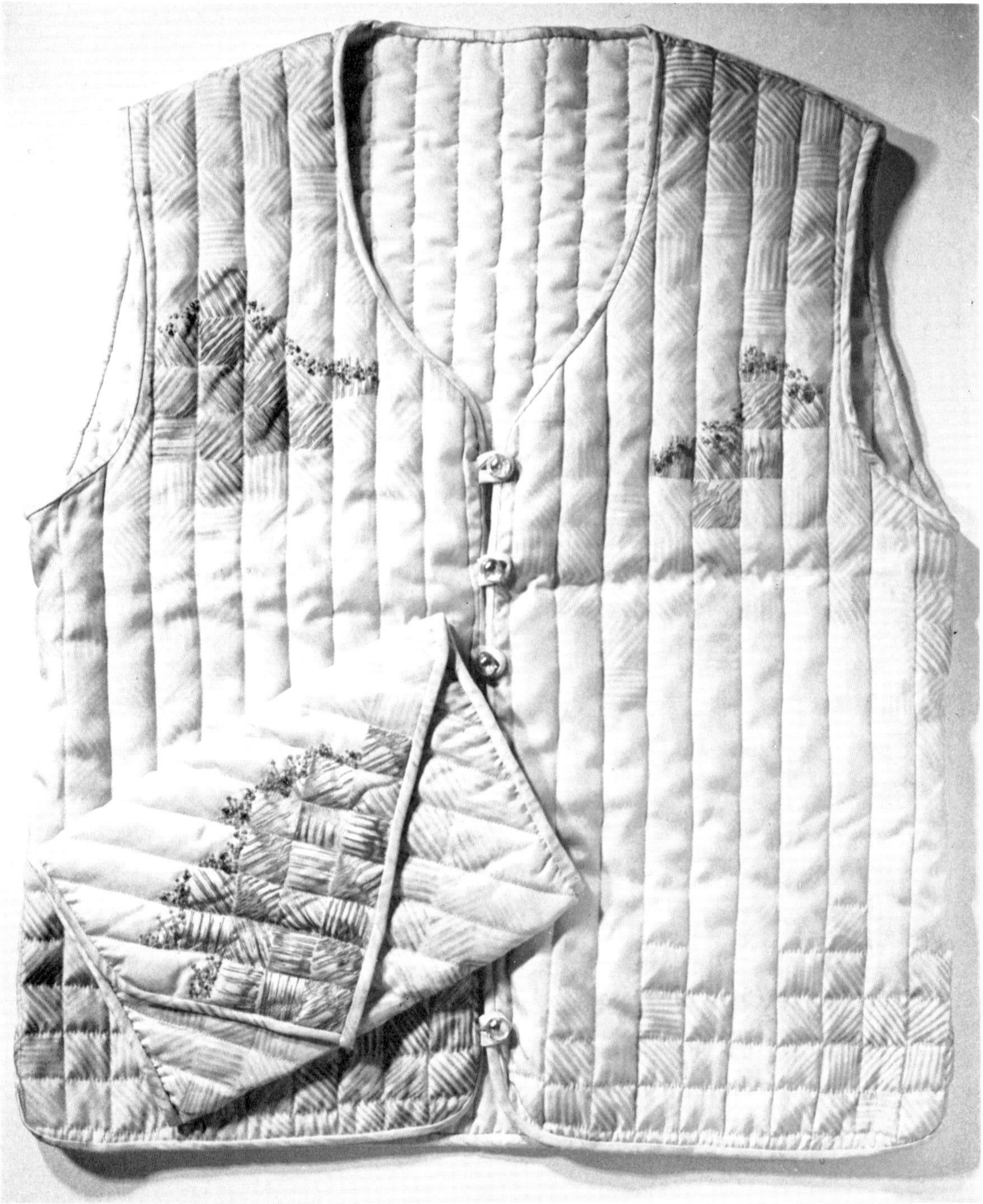

Fig. 7. A beautifully designed waistcoat and matching bag. Fabric transfer pencils were used to print the geometric design on the fabric. The waistcoat has been machine quilted and areas of surface stitchery added (Denise Journeaux)

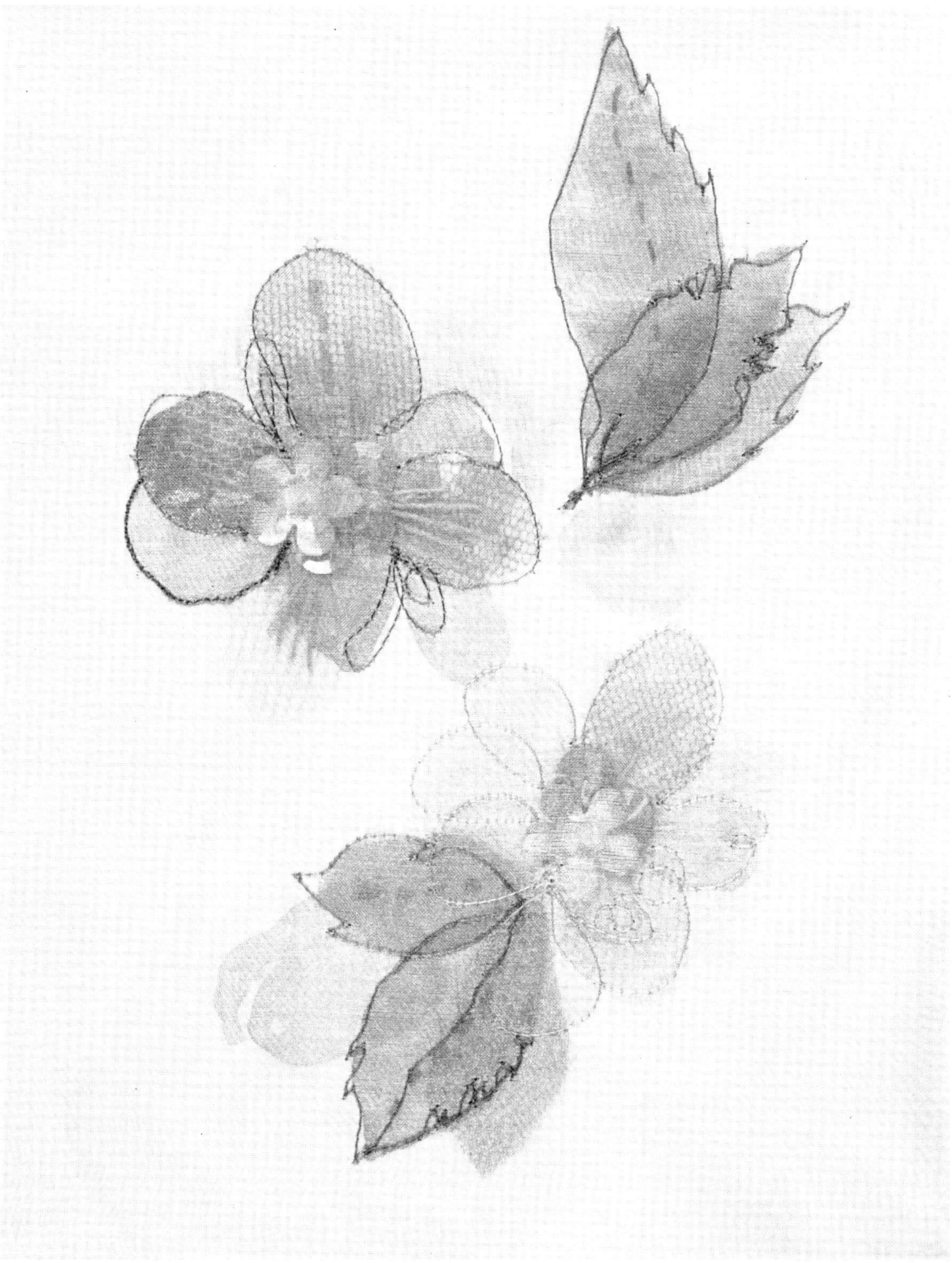

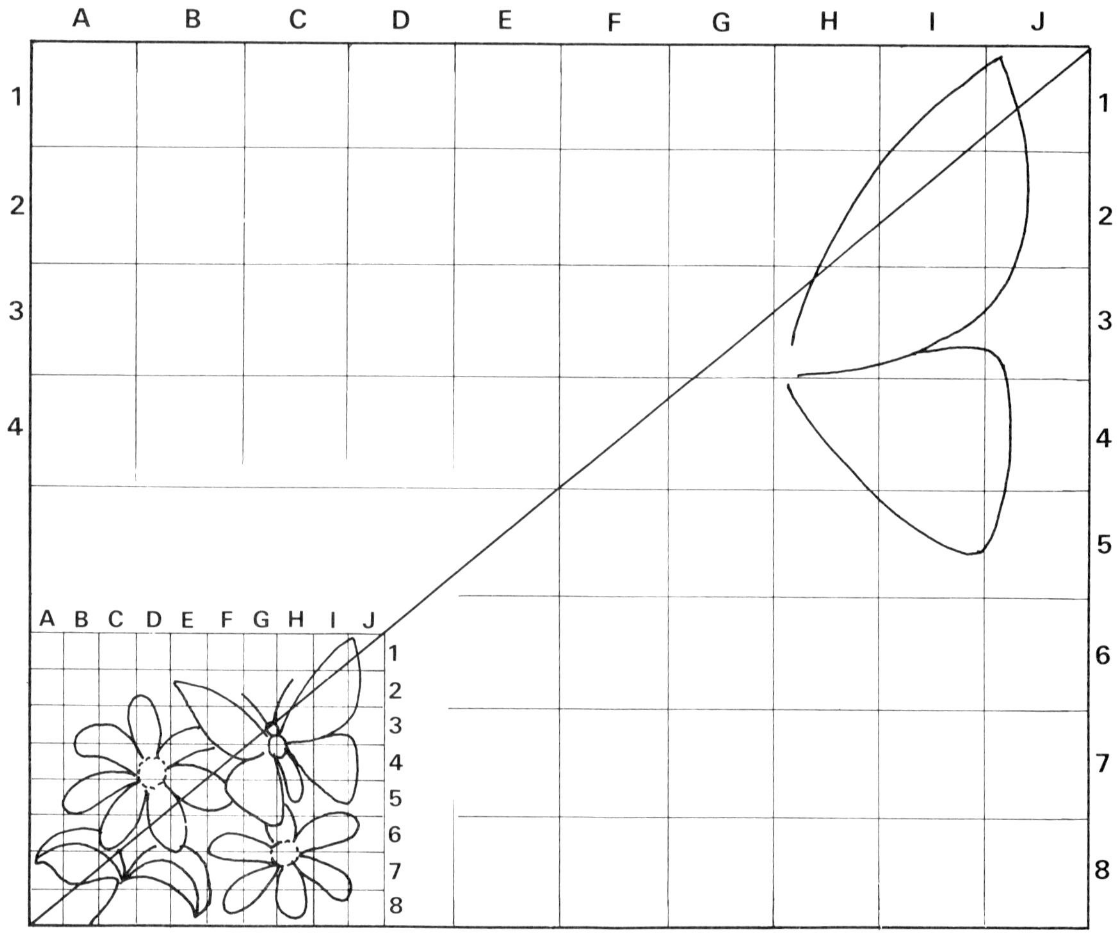

fabric, and transfer crayons are also available. The pens tend to be quite expensive, whereas the crayons can be bought very cheaply and are good for experiments.

Collect together a variety of different types of fabric and try some of the following experiments. Limit your choice of fabric paints to the three primary colours, and mix them to obtain other colours.

1. Make a stencil by cutting a simple shape in the centre of a piece of card. Place the stencil on the fabric and spray through the hole with fabric paint. Either use a spray diffuser (available at art shops), or splatter with an old toothbrush dipped in paint (remember to wear rubber gloves). When the fabric is dry, move the stencil so that the new shape overlaps the first, and spray again, preferably in a different colour.
2. Make similar experiments using the shape that you cut away from the card, spraying around the template, and overlapping the shapes.
3. Experiment with the paints to make background fabrics for embroideries. Dampen the fabric first before sponging the colour into the fabric. (Be careful not to overload the fabric with colour.)

Fig. 8. Flowers transfer painted on an opaque background fabric. Sheer fabric was placed on top and tiny pieces of net and organza sandwiched between the two layers. The petals are outlined with fine couched threads (Barbara Mellor)

Fig. 9. Enlarging a design using a graph

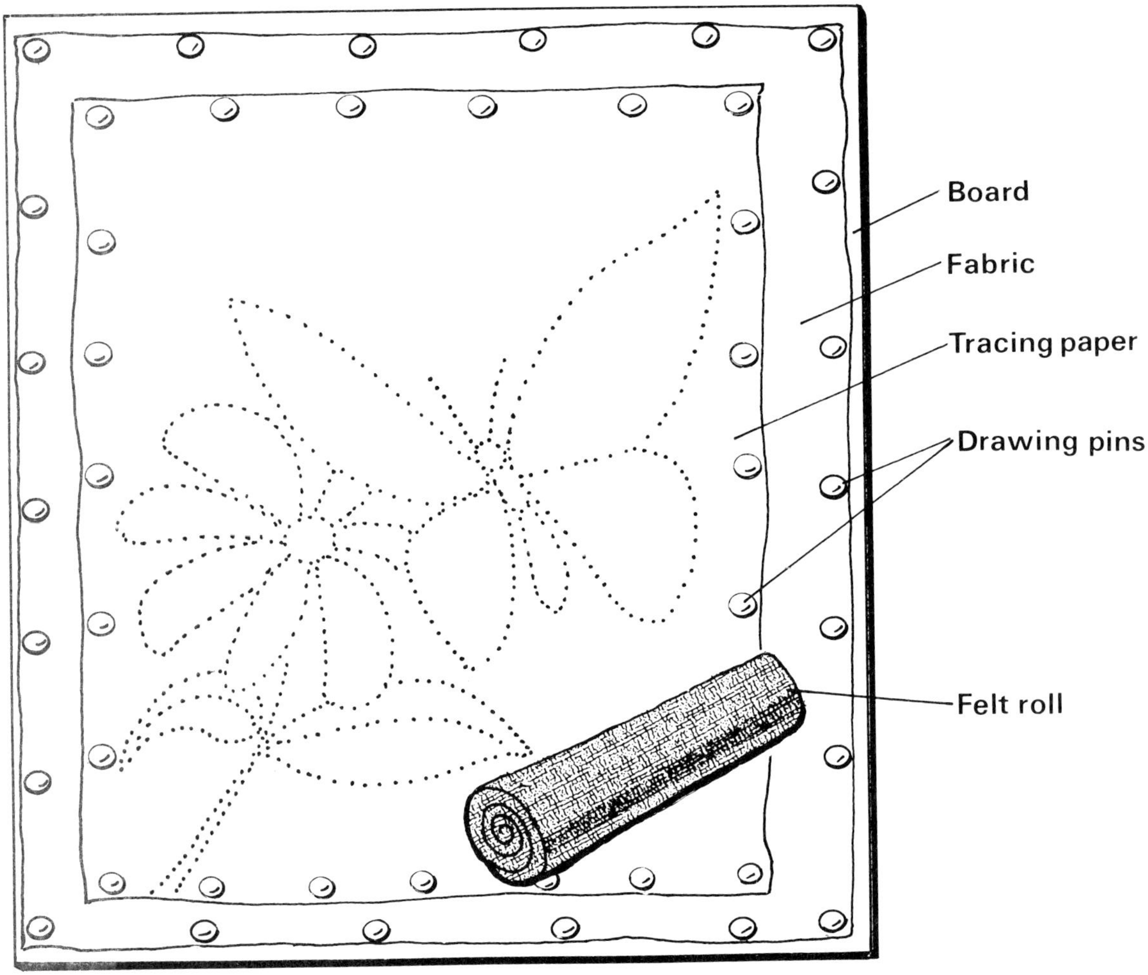

Fig. 10. The prick and pounce method of transferring designs to the fabric

Car spray paints can also be used successfully, although they tend to stiffen the fabric. They should be used out of doors, on a still day, and preferably while wearing a mask. Other suggestions for using fabric paint can be found in the following chapters.

Enlarging designs

It is useful to know how to enlarge (or reduce) a design suitable for embroidery. The easiest way is to use a photocopier that has enlarging facilities. However, if one is not available, instructions are given below:

1. Trace the design on tracing paper (greaseproof paper is suitable for this) and draw a rectangle or square around the design.
2. Divide the shape into equal squares (e.g. 1 inch, 2.5 cm) and number each square horizontally and vertically.
3. Secure the drawing in the bottom left-hand corner of a large sheet of drawing paper.
4. Draw a diagonal line across the tracing, extending it to the edge of the larger sheet.
5. Decide on the size of the enlarged design and extend the bottom line of the original design to the required length. From this point, draw a vertical line at right angles to the first until it

meets the extended diagonal line. Draw in the other lines on the large sheet.

6. Count the number of squares on the smaller design and divide the large sheet into exactly the same number. Number them identically.
7. Working in one square at a time, carefully copy the lines of the small design into the corresponding squares on the larger paper. The design will then be ready to transfer to fabric.

Transferring designs to fabric

There are several methods of transferring designs to fabric, some very simple, and others more complicated.

1. For simple shapes, perhaps to make repeat patterns, a template can be used. Transfer the motif to stiff paper and pin carefully to the background fabric. Using small stitches and tacking cotton, tack carefully all around the edge of the card. Remove the template and repeat when needed.

   Water soluble markers are now available, and could be used to draw lightly around the design. These should be used with extreme care, however, as they have a tendency to reappear after they have been washed away and it is believed that the chemicals they contain will rot the fabric in time. If you do use them, they should be carefully washed away with clean, fresh cold tap-water. An alternative to the soluble marker is a water-soluble crayon in a pale colour.

   When using this technique for quilting, the design can be traced with the point of a stiletto or chenille needle. This will leave an indented image that will last long enough to complete the quilting.
2. For more elaborate designs, take a tracing of the design and pin it to the background fabric. Using small stitches, carefully sew through all the lines of the design. When this has been completed, the tracing can be carefully torn away. The tacking should be removed as the embroidery progresses.
3. For canvas work, the design can be traced directly on to the canvas by laying the canvas over the design. Always use a waterproof pen.
4. The prick and pounce method is used for intricate designs. It is quite time-consuming, but very effective. You will need powdered chalk for dark fabrics and charcoal for light materials. Powdered cinnamon can also be used and works quite well on darkish fabrics. You will also need a piece of rolled felt, tracing paper, a stiletto, a fine brush and water-colour paint.
   a. Trace the design on tracing paper and lay face down on a padded surface. Using a stiletto or large needle with the eye stuck firmly into a cork, prick holes through the design, about $\frac{1}{4}$ inch (5 mm) apart.
   b. Lay the tracing right side up on the background fabric and secure with pins.
   c. Take the rolled felt and carefully rub the chalk or charcoal all over the design. Carefully remove the tracing.
   d. With a very fine brush and water-colour paint, join all the dots together to form the embroidery design.

Two

Making stitches work

Surface stitches play a vital part in contemporary embroidery. Linear stitches, such as running, stem or chain stitch, can be used to build up areas of intricate pattern. Other stitches, such as french knots or seeding, can be massed together to create textures or used to break up areas of plain background.

It is better to know how to work a few stitches really well, than to acquire a scant knowledge of many. A good stitch dictionary is an essential part of the embroiderer's equipment.

In the past, samplers were worked, usually by young girls as their first piece of embroidery, in order to perfect stitches. These samplers were usually very structured and formal. Today, samplers still play a very important role, providing the embroiderer with an opportunity to experiment with stitches, fabrics and threads.

Collect together a variety of threads, from fine sewing cotton to knitting yarn. An assortment of different sized needles will also be required to accommodate the differing thicknesses of thread. Stitch samples can be worked on calico or similar fabric, held in a ring frame. However, a more loosely woven fabric, such as hessian, is best suited to thicker threads.

Illustrated in this chapter there are a few stitches which the beginner may find useful. However, there are many more to be tried out, which can be found in dictionaries.

Playing with stitches

To begin, choose one of the stitches described here. Use a medium weight thread, such as coton à broder or stranded cotton. Do not cut a length of thread longer than about 18 inches (45 cm), or it will become unmanageable. Choose a needle with a sharp point through which the thread may easily travel. Start with a knot on the wrong side of the fabric.

It is important to know how to work the stitch correctly before you begin to play with it! If it is a linear stitch, try working it in rows, carefully and regularly, making sure that the stitches are all fairly equal in length. When you are confident of your ability to work the stitches correctly, you can begin to experiment with them.

Use different thicknesses of thread – stitch with fine sewing cotton next to a very thick wool. Try glossy threads, smooth, matt threads and hairy threads of all thicknesses. Narrow ribbons, string, and fabric cut into strips can all be utilised and all provide different textural effects.

Vary the size of the stitch. Use an assortment of threads and make very large stitches next to tiny ones.

Overlap stitches to build up a thick, solid texture. Sew different weights and different textured threads on top of one another.

Work some stitches close together and others far apart. Vary the direction of the stitch. For

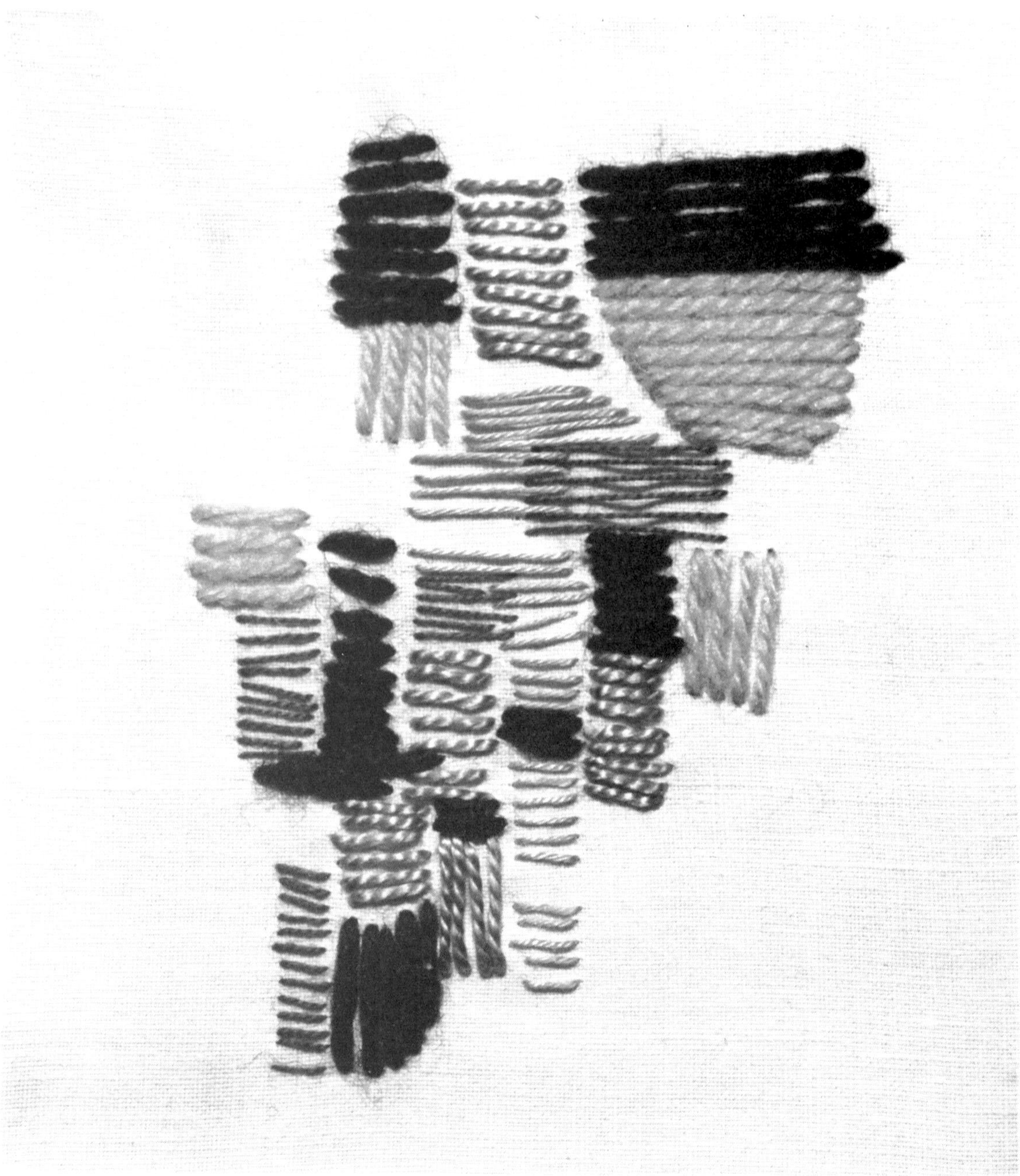

Fig. 11. Stitch sampler showing blocks of straight stitches worked in a variety of threads, some shiny, others smooth (Barbara Mellor)

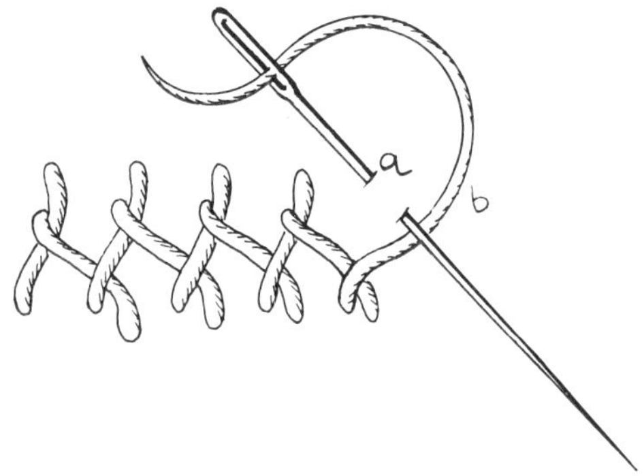

Fig. 12. Cretan stitch is worked from left to right. Insert the needle into the fabric at A. Bring out at B, with the thread lying underneath the point of the needle. Then repeat, re-inserting the needle at B and bringing it out at C

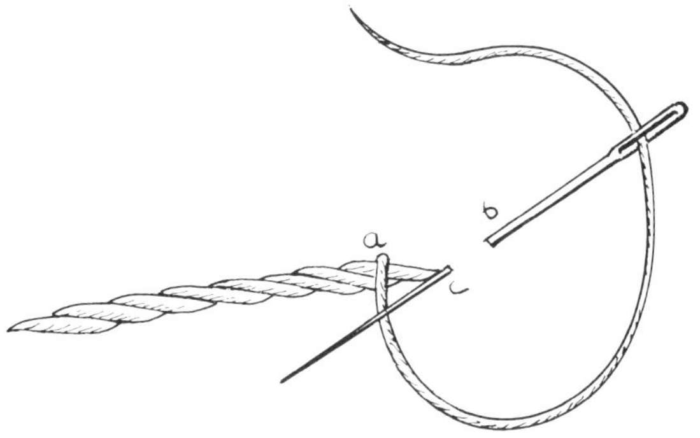

Fig. 14. Stem stitch is worked from left to right. Bring the needle up through the fabric at A and re-insert at B. Bring the needle up again at C, so that the stitches form an overlapping line

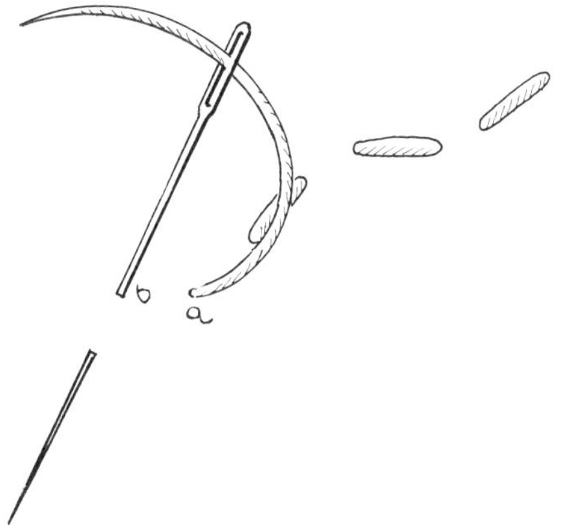

Fig. 13. Running stitch is worked from right to left. Bring the needle up through the fabric at A and re-insert at B. With a little practice, several stitches may be worked before pulling the thread completely through the fabric

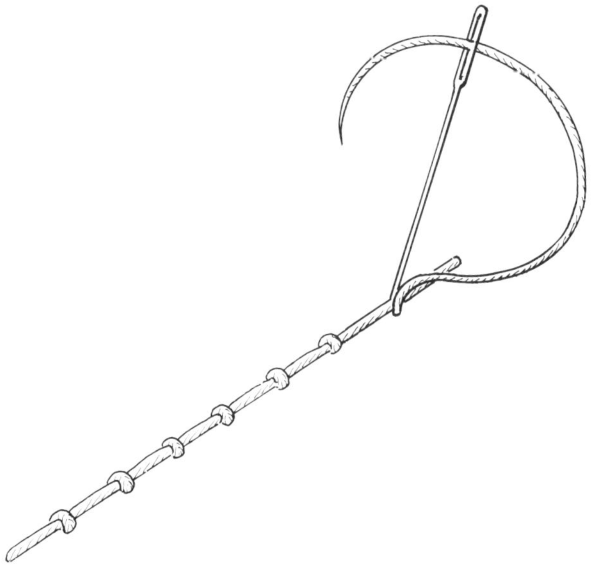

Fig. 15. Couching. The thread to be couched is first laid on the fabric and held in place by tiny stitches, usually sewn at right angles to the couched thread. The couching stitches can be angled if required, or other stitches, such as cross stitch or detached chain, used. The couched threads can be smooth, but textured threads give interesting effects

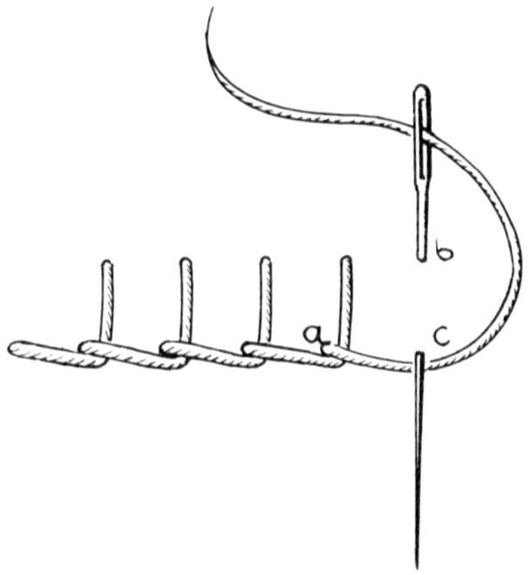

Fig. 16. Buttonhole stitch is worked from left to right. Bring the needle up through the fabric at A. Re-insert at B and bring up through the fabric again at C, with the thread lying underneath the needle

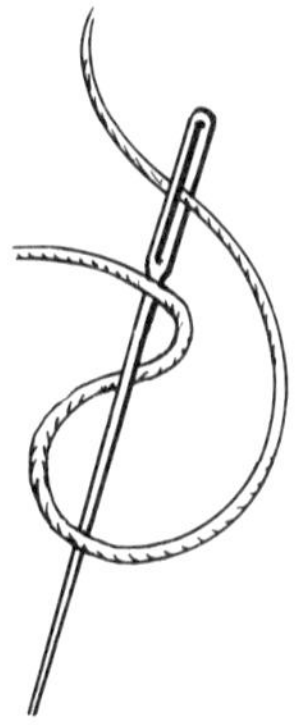

Fig. 17. French knots. Bring the needle up through the fabric and twist the thread twice around the needle. Re-insert the needle close to where it emerged, pulling the thread carefully through the knot to the wrong side of the fabric

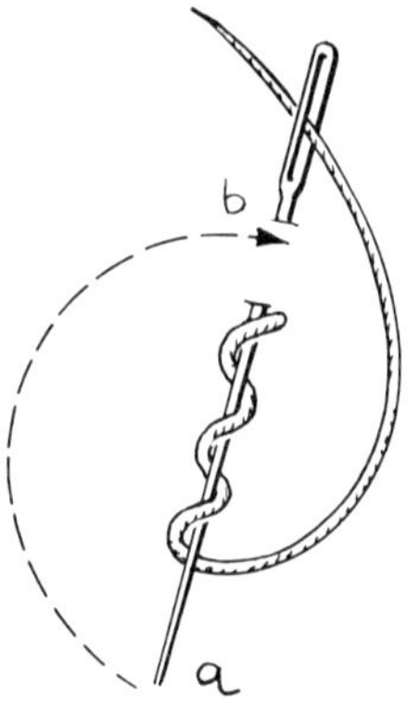

Fig. 18. Bullion knots. Bring the needle up through the fabric at A and re-insert at B. Twist the thread approximately six or seven times around the needle. Carefully pull the needle through the fabric and threads. Re-insert the needle in fabric at A. Bullion knots can be quite a difficult stitch to work but are worth the effort. Use a smooth thread, such as coton à broder, rather than one which is tightly twisted

instance, straight stitches worked in blocks using the same coloured thread will reflect the light at different angles and produce a range of tones of one colour.

Keep all your samplers for future reference, making careful notes of stitches and threads.

Designing for stitchery

Natural objects make a good starting point. Look for interesting textures on tree bark, a leaf, shell or pebble. A good way to start designing is by taking rubbings. Use thin paper and a child's wax crayon. Lay the paper carefully over the object you have chosen and rub gently with the crayon, making sure that you work in one direction only.

Work a small piece of embroidery from the rubbing. At this stage, it is probably better to keep to a simple colour scheme–perhaps shades of one colour. Collect a variety of thicknesses of thread. Use a good tempered background and mount it in a ring frame. Limit yourself to only two or three stitches.

Stitch directly on to the fabric, using the rubbing as your inspiration. Look carefully at the

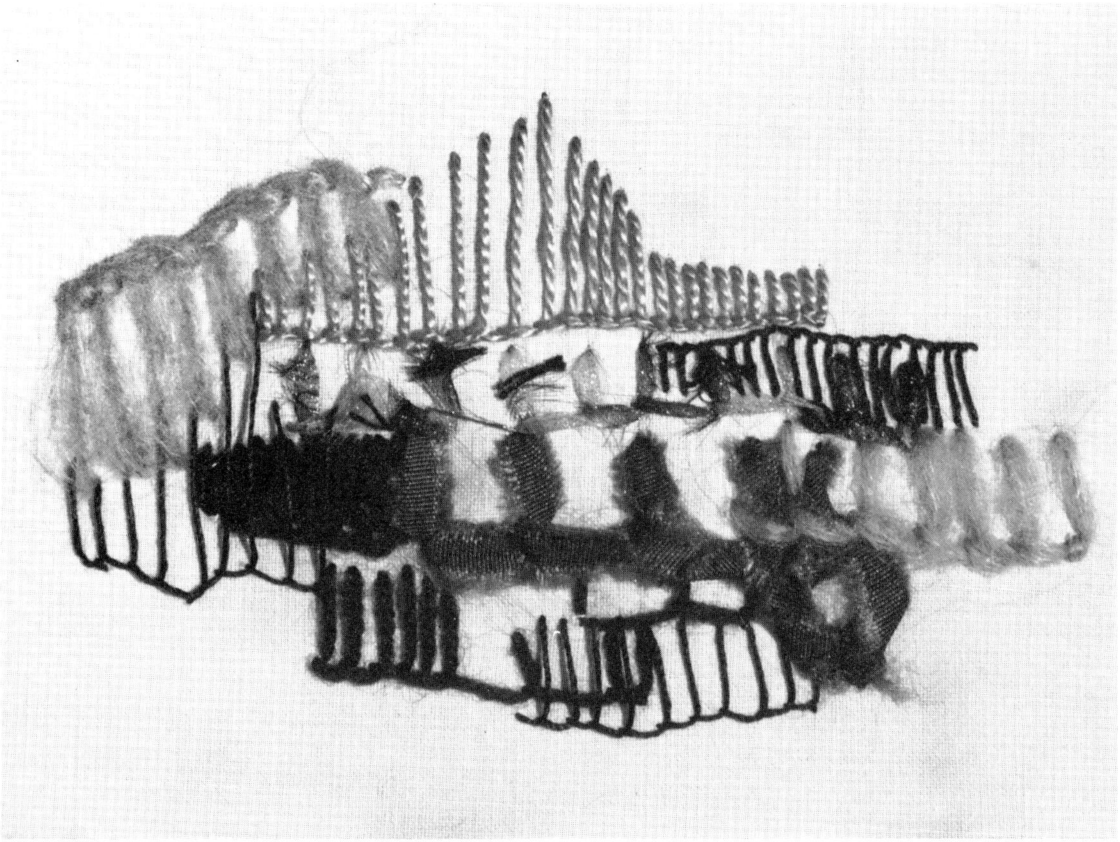

Fig. 19. Buttonhole stitch sampler, using different threads, including torn fabric strips (Barbara Mellor)

marks made on the rubbing and try to interpret them as stitchery. Begin by building up the overall structure of your design, instead of concentrating on one small area. There may be radiating lines of the rubbing that can be worked as linear stitches. When the design begins to take shape, detail can be added. For instance, areas of texture might be built up as knots or seeding.

From time to time, take a step back from your work and look at it with a critical eye–try to have calm areas within the embroidery, perhaps plain, unworked background fabric to complement a mass of thick stitchery, otherwise the embroidery will look very busy. Do not be discouraged if your first results are disappointing. Keep practising your stitches and your work will steadily improve.

Printing and embroidery

Collect together a variety of textured objects, such as corks, leaves or pieces of sponge, that could be used to print on fabric. Potatoes can be halved and carved into a simple printing block. Apples and other fruit can be halved and used successfully. Use fabric paints and print directly on to the fabric. Be careful not to overload the block; it is quite useful to have a pad of felt soaked with the paint. Push the block into the pad and then press once on to the fabric.

After experimenting to obtain the right consistency of paint, build up patterns with your block. Print rows side by side or directly beneath each other. Make half drop and spot patterns. Make simple border designs, with overlapping blocks.

When the fabric is dry, iron on the wrong side to set the paint. Then use stitchery to add interest to the design and create an all-over pattern. When using printed fabrics, quite often it is the background that needs to be embroidered and the printed shapes left unadorned. Consider using linear stitches, such as chain or back stitch, to make up simple grids between the prints.

Working from photographs

When you have enough confidence in your ability, make a small embroidered panel. Photographs provide a good source of inspiration; they can be of gardens, buildings, landscapes, flowers, etc. Choose a subject that has fairly simple shapes. If the photograph is particularly busy, cut out a frame in a piece of thin card and isolate one area.

Fig. 20. Cretan stitch sampler, using various threads, including narrow ribbon. Some of the stitches have been worked quite close together and others stretched further apart (Barbara Mellor)

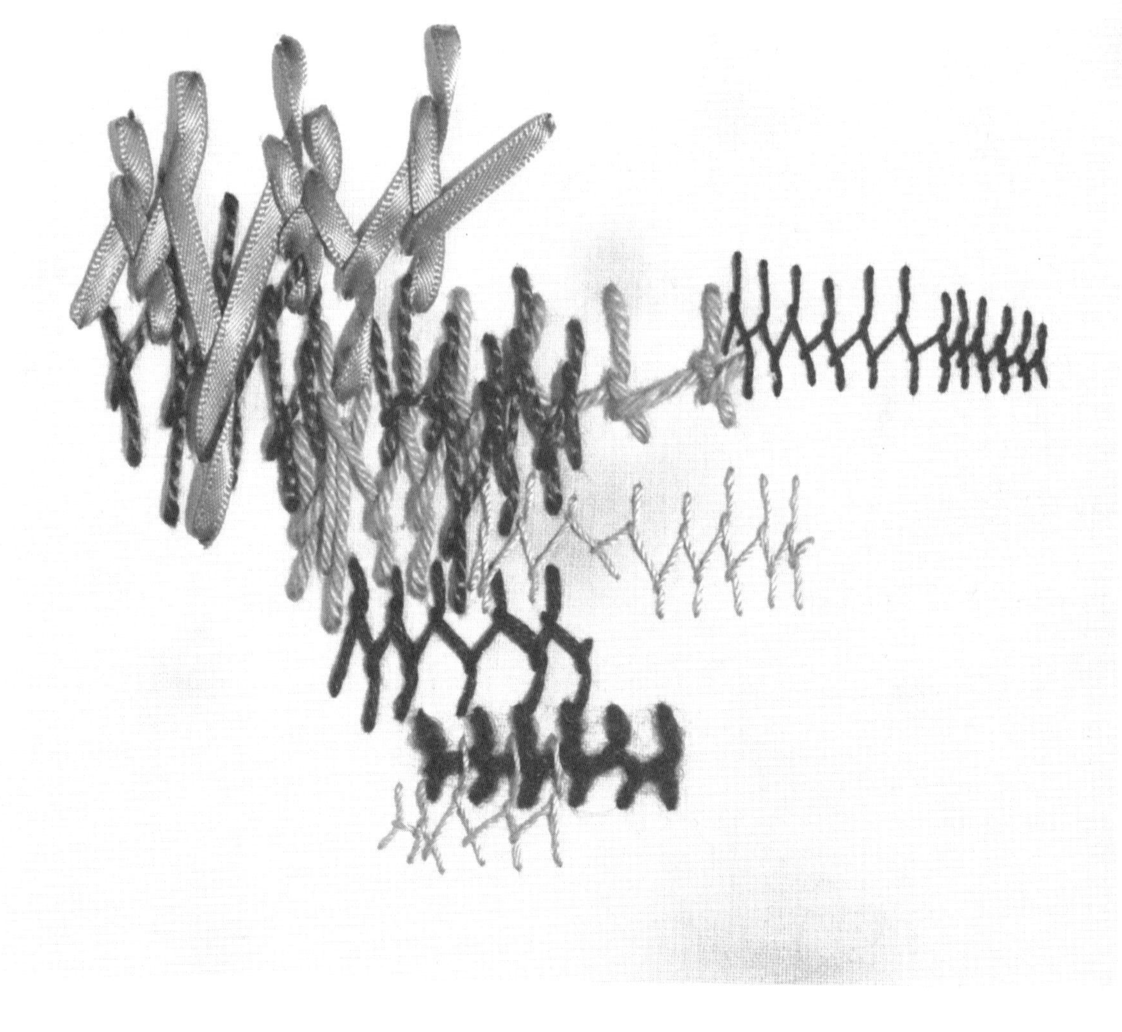

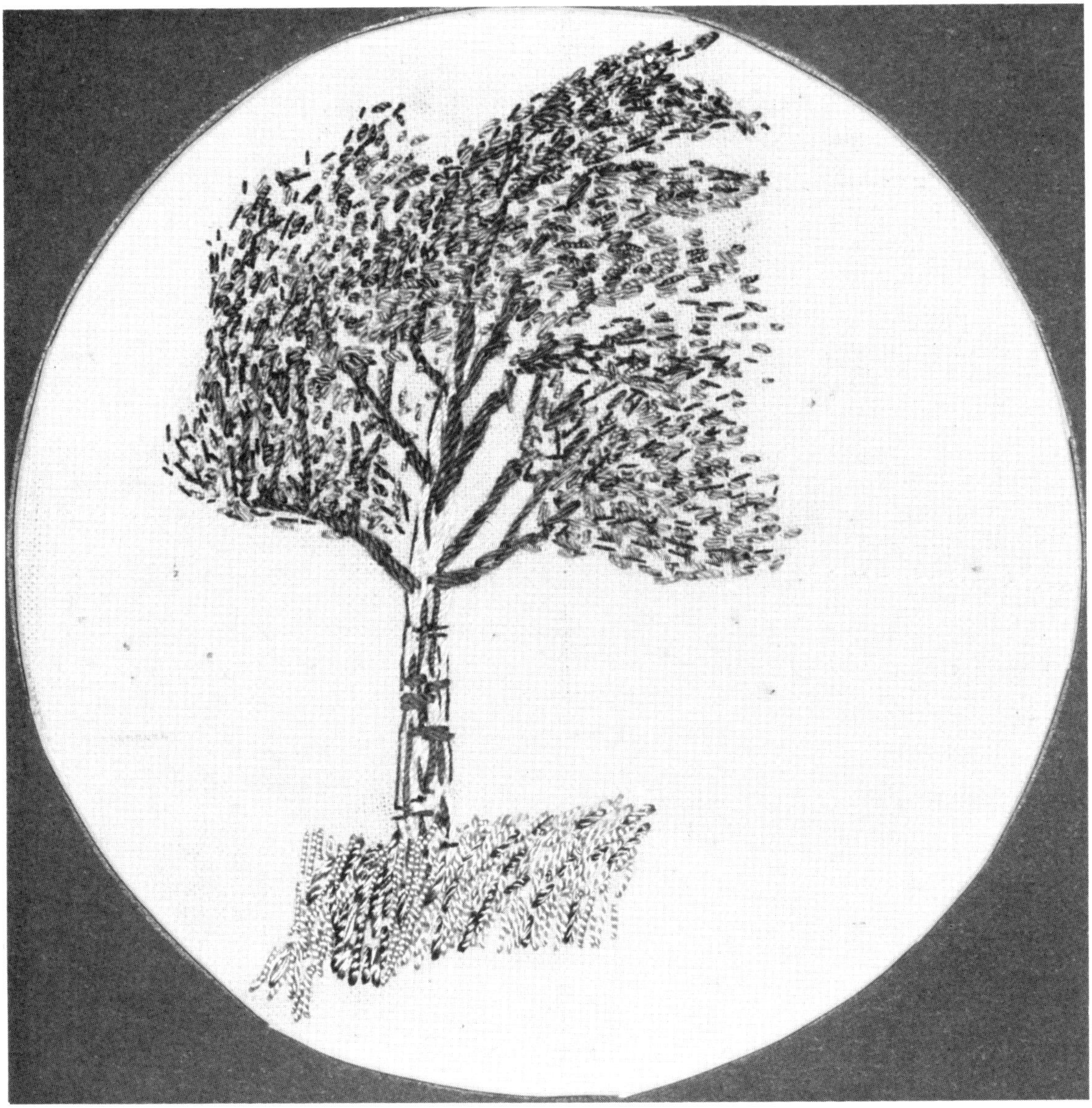

Fig. 21. Tree, worked mainly in small running stitches and depicting a good sense of movement (Frances Roche)

Decide on the size of the panel and background fabric to be used. Calico is perfectly suitable. If the panel is small enough the fabric can probably be placed in a ring frame. If not, it will need to be mounted on a square frame (see Chapter 1 for instructions).

Choose a colour scheme and collect some threads. The photograph may suggest appropriate colours. If not, try one of the suggestions given in Chapter 3 in the paragraph on colour. In either case, beware of using too many colours, especially if the embroidery is to be small.

Trace the outlines of the main shapes of your photograph on thin paper and transfer them to the background fabric.

You may wish to use fabric paint to obtain background colour, especially if the thought of getting started is rather daunting. Dampen the fabric and lightly sponge in diluted colour. Do not make the colour too heavy, as it will dominate the whole design. Allow to dry and iron on the wrong side. Alternatively, the background can be sprayed with a mouth diffuser or spattered with an old toothbrush dipped in paint.

Once again, start by building up the main outlines of the design. Ensure that you plan a focal point–the part of the embroidery to which the eye is immediately drawn. There are several ways to obtain this–perhaps by using a spot of brilliant or complementary colour. Or try a very busy area surrounded by a quiet space or an empty space; massed stitchery in shiny threads next to stitches worked in smooth threads.

Remember to stand back from your work and regard it with a critical eye. It is often helpful to

Fig. 22. A herb pillow, based on the verse, 'When daisies pied ... '. Worked on a painted background, with very dense stitchery in places. The verse has been embroidered around the edge of the pillow (Diana Mitchell)

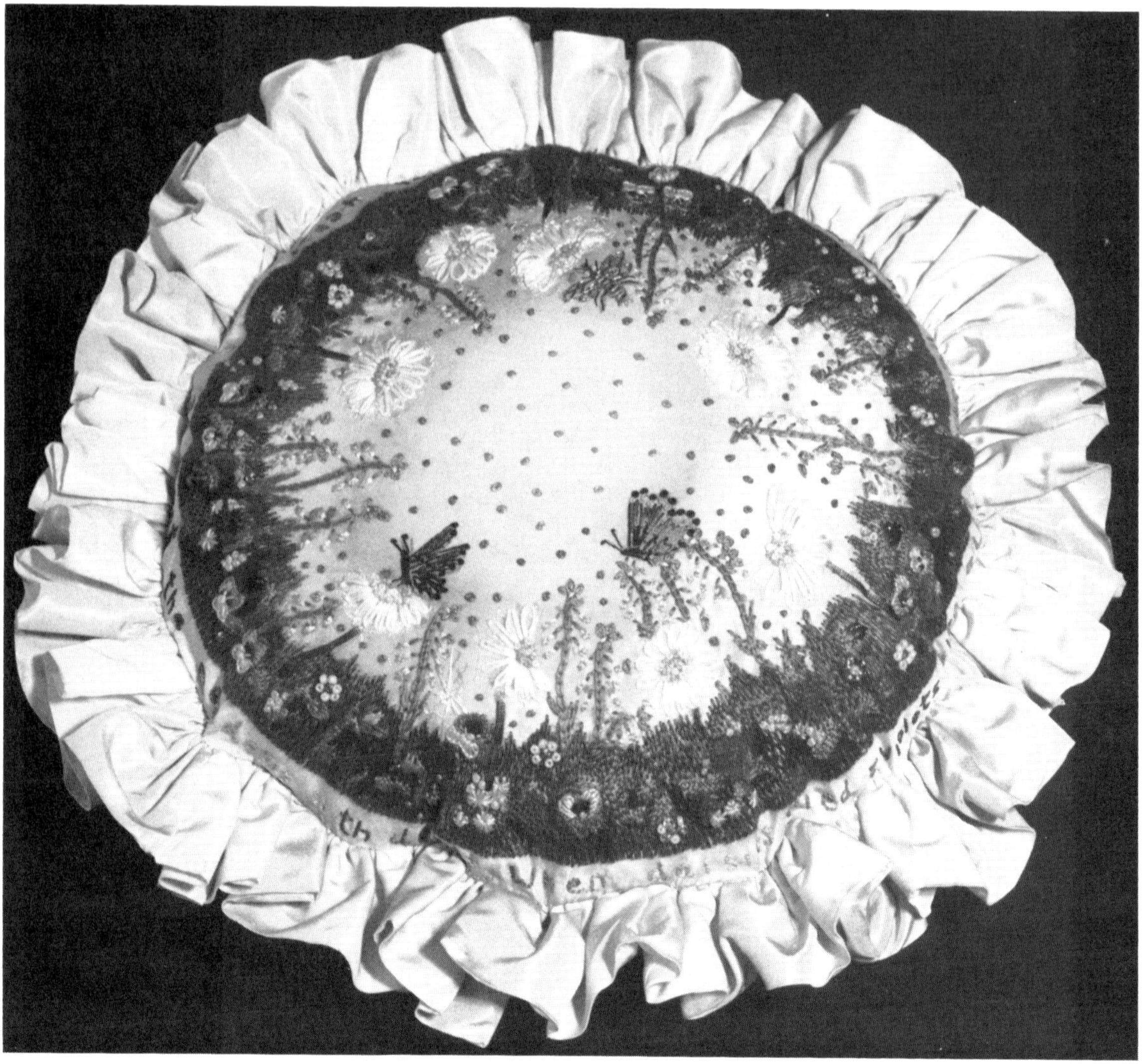

make a card frame to place around the embroidery. Keep the stitchery fairly simple–avoid too much colour and too many stitches.

As the work progresses, keep working on it as a whole, rather than becoming too caught up in areas of concentrated texture. Make sure that the focal point remains the most important part of the design. Remember to use the stitches to interpret your design.

When you have finished the embroidery to your satisfaction, stretch it and mount it over card (Chapter 8). If desired, it could be placed in a simple, purchased frame.

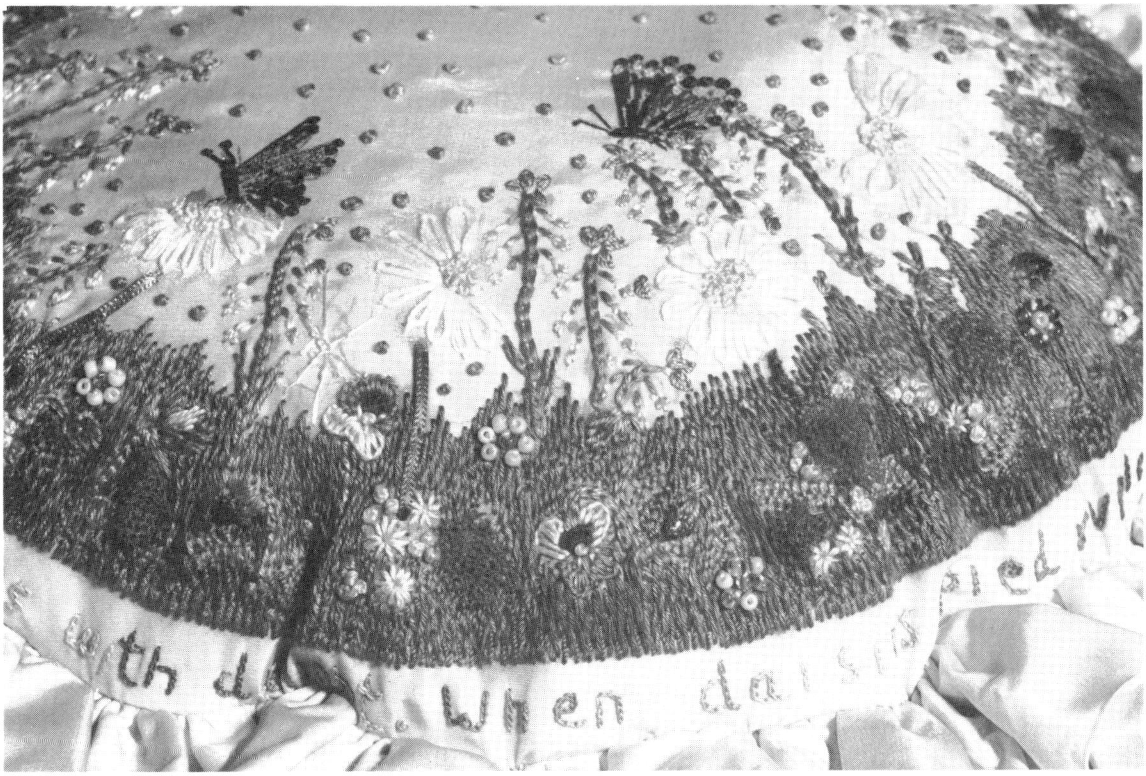

Fig. 23. Detail of Fig. 22. Cretan stitch has been worked very close together to give the appearance of foliage. The flowers are worked in eyelet stitch or detached chain. Other stitches include french knots, chain and straight stitch (Diana Mitchell)

Fig. 24. A moth, worked in fine silks, using blocks of quite regular straight stitches to build up the design (Muriel Best)

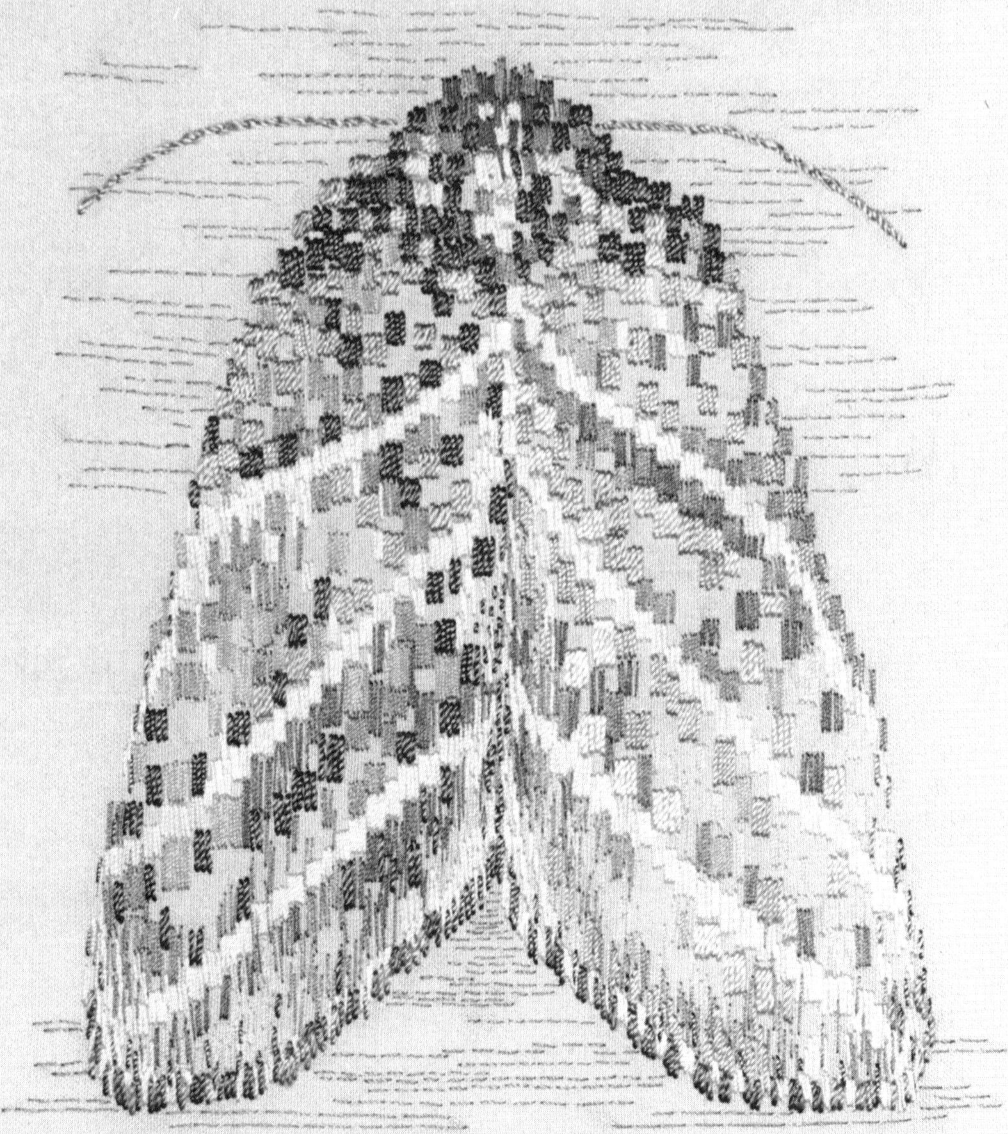

Three

Shadow work and colour

Shadow work developed in the nineteenth century, probably as a result of the importation of fine cotton muslin from India. It has similarities to a form of Indian embroidery called Chikan work, which combines shadow work with surface stitchery and areas of open work. Shadow embroidery was used to decorate clothing, especially lingerie, and household articles that did not require a lot of laundering–tray cloths, tea cosies, etc.

Fabrics

Traditionally, cotton organdie has been used, but any light, transparent fabric will do–e.g. nylon, silk organza, voile. Threads are traditionally white and suitable types are coton à broder, fine silks and stranded cotton.

Transferring the design

This can be done using the tracing and tacking method. Alternatively, the design can be transferred directly to the fabric with a washable crayon, or with water-colour and a fine brush.

Frames

It is not neccessary to use a frame, but you will probably find it easier if you do.

Design sources

Traditionally, floral designs with long, flowing stems and graceful leaves were used. These designs are still very apt for modern shadow work. Instead of taking tracings from photographs in a book, make your own drawings from flowers in your garden. Keep to simple shapes, such as snowdrops, daffodils and aquilegia. Remember that it is not terribly important to obtain beautiful, anatomically correct drawings, but aim at simple sketches to capture the important elements of the flower. When you have achieved a design that pleases you, transfer it to fabric. Cotton organdie is a good fabric to begin with: it is quite crisp and easy to handle.

Embroidery

In shadow work, the embroidery is always worked on the reverse side of the fabric. The stitch used most often is closed herringbone. If worked correctly, this will appear on the front of the work as two parallel rows of back stitch with shadowy

Fig. 25. Shadow embroidery, based on plant drawings. The leaf shapes have been cut out of sheer fabric and applied to the reverse of the background fabric with Bondaweb and outlined in running stitch. Other leaves are worked in herringbone stitch and the stem in back stitch (Jenny Bullen)

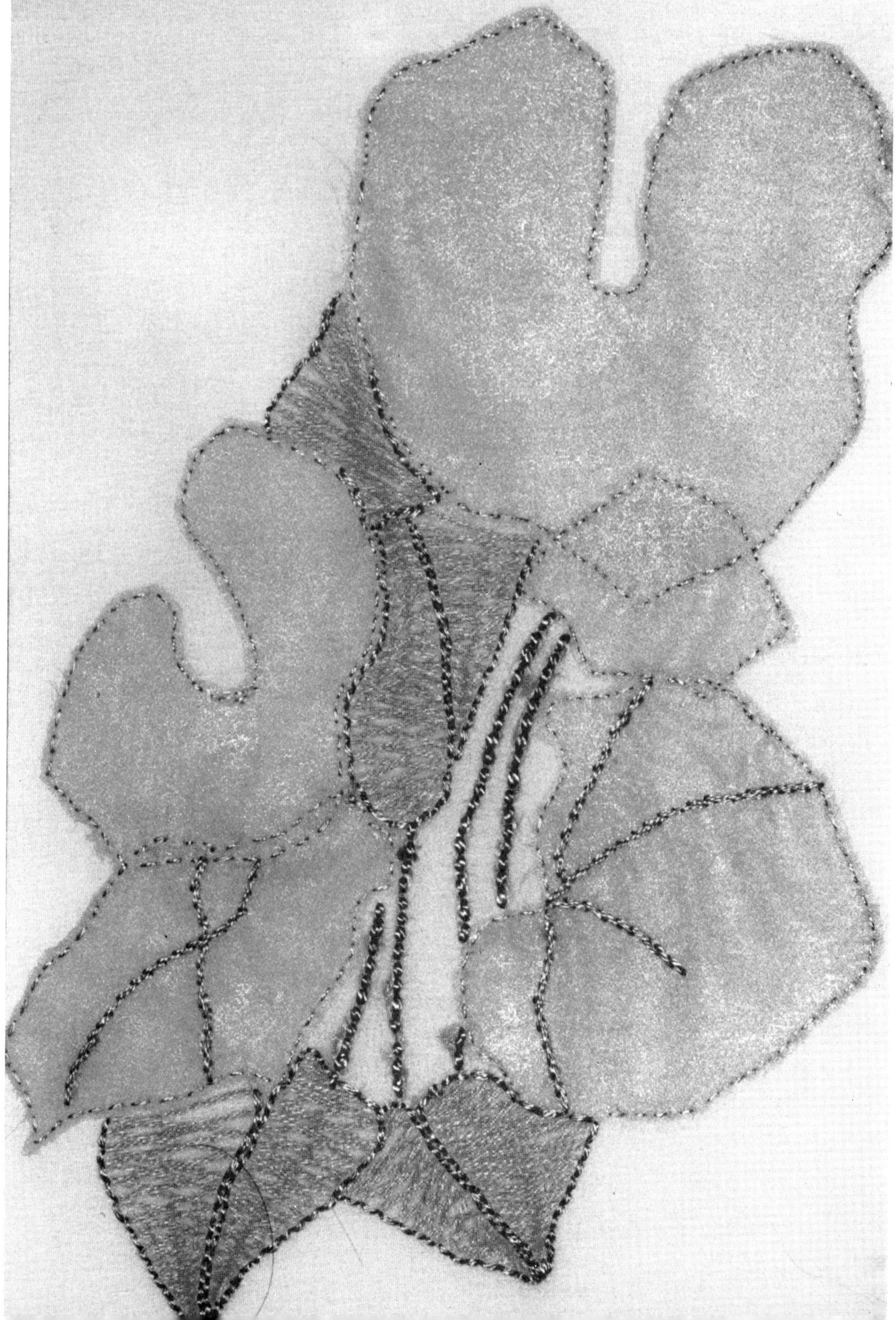

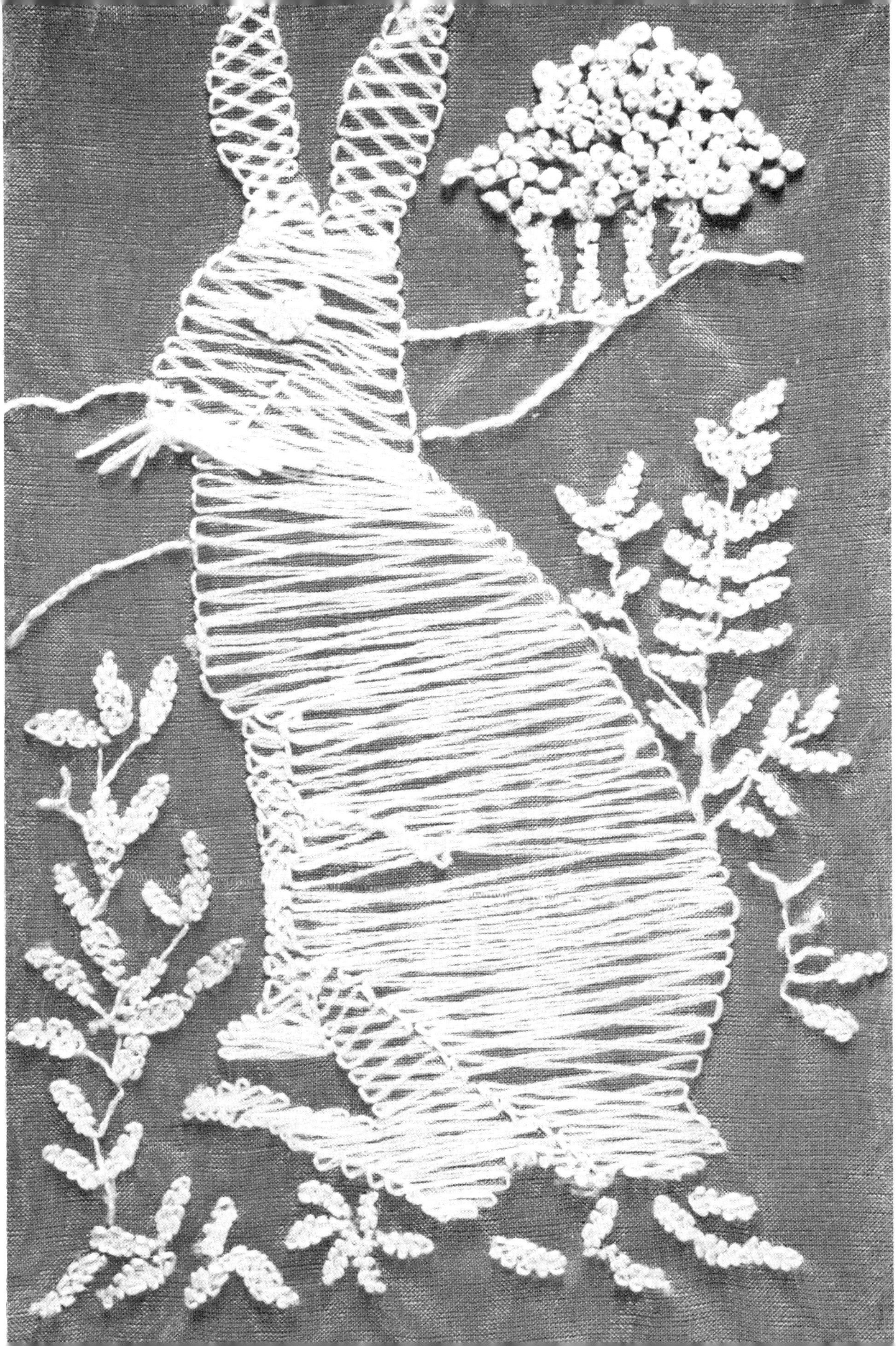

cris-crossed lines between. Other stitches can, of course, be used to add interest to the design. Double back stitch could be used instead of herringbone, when a single line of stitchery is required; the french knots and bullion knots to add surface texture. For a rather more solid effect, pieces of organdie can be applied to the design. They should be tacked to the reverse and held in place with pin stitch or three-sided stitch.

Experiment with colour

Pastel colours have often been used with shadow work: for instance, a coloured thread could be used on white fabric, or areas of coloured appliqué behind the ground fabric. However, experimenting with colour and interesting fabrics makes shadow work a much more interesting technique for present day embroidery.

Some people find choosing and mixing colours quite an easy task, while others find it much more difficult. Choice is, of course, very much a personal matter. However, every embroiderer will find it beneficial to know some of the rules of colour theory and how to use them to add interest to her embroidery.

The three 'primary' colours are red, blue and yellow. Each should be a very clear, pure colour and contain no hint of the other two.
'Secondary' colours are obtained by mixing together portions of primary colours. Yellow and red create orange; yellow and blue green; and red and blue violet.
'Complementary colours' are pairs of colours opposite each other on the colour circle, i.e. yellow and violet, red and green, and blue and orange.
'Tertiary' colours are obtained by mixing a secondary colour with a primary.
'Tone' describes how light or dark a colour is.
'Shade' is the pure colour mixed with black to make it darker.

Fig. 26. A rabbit in shadow work. Although the stitchery has been worked on the reverse of the fabric, it stands out quite sharply because the fabric used is very sheer (Diana Mitchell)

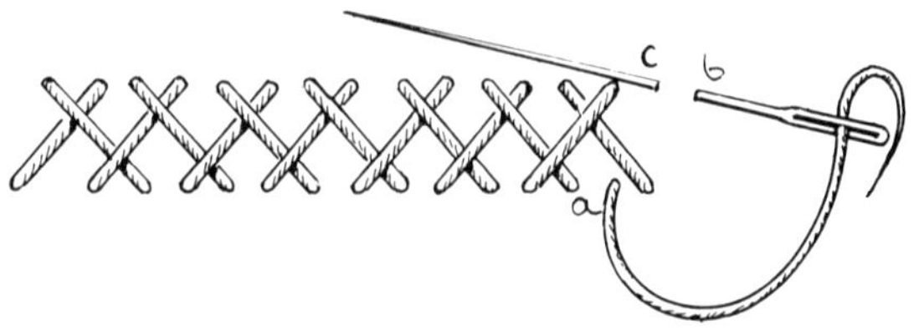

Fig. 27. Herringbone stitch, worked from left to right. Bring the needle up at A. Re-insert the needle at D and out again at E. When used in shadow work, the stitch is worked on the wrong side of the fabric so that only two parallel rows of back stitching appear on the front

'Tint' is the pure colour mixed with white to make it paler.
'Analogous' colours are a range of colours that adjoin each other on the colour circle, i.e. blues to violets, or green to yellow and orange.
A 'monochromatic' colour scheme consists of one colour only, plus its tints and shades.
'Warm' colours are reds, oranges and yellows. These colours always appear to 'come forward' when used. 'Cool' colours are blues and greens. Blues usually appear to recede.
A 'harmonious' colour scheme is one that always seems to 'go together', or be comfortable. Analogous colours will always produce a harmonious colour range. They can, however, have a tendency to be rather dull, or safe, and it is always worth experimenting, perhaps by using a brilliant spot of a complementary colour to 'lift' your work.

Colour observation

A good way to choose a colour scheme for your embroideries is by observing natural or man-made objects. Select some things that appeal to you–shells or pebbles, flowers from the garden, foliage from the hedgerow, bricks or a wooden fence, tree bark or a log. Carefully record your observations in a sketchbook. Aim to match your colour studies exactly to the colours on the object you are looking at. Use a variety of media to produce this–paints or scraps of fabric glued in place, or threads wrapped over a small piece of card.

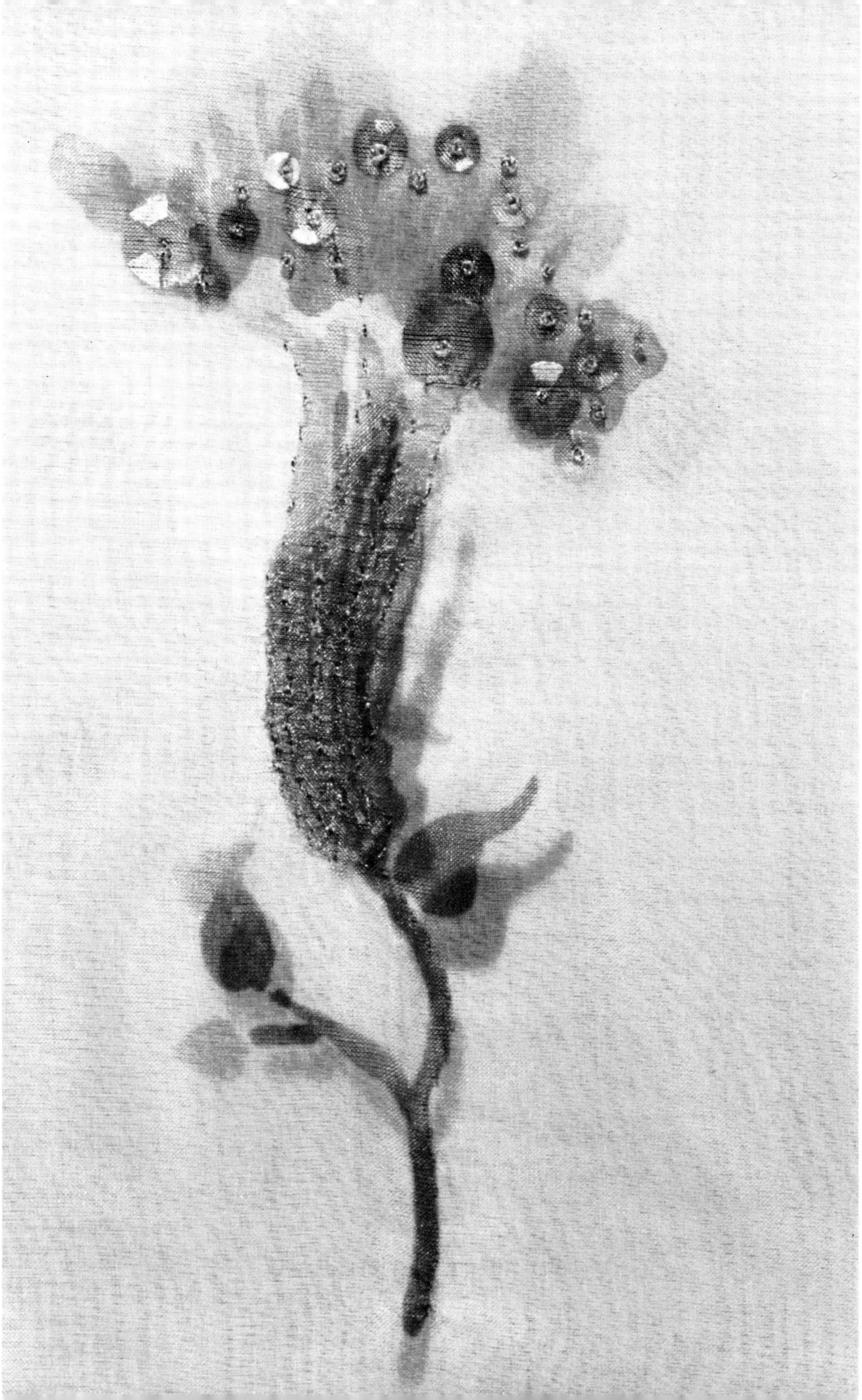

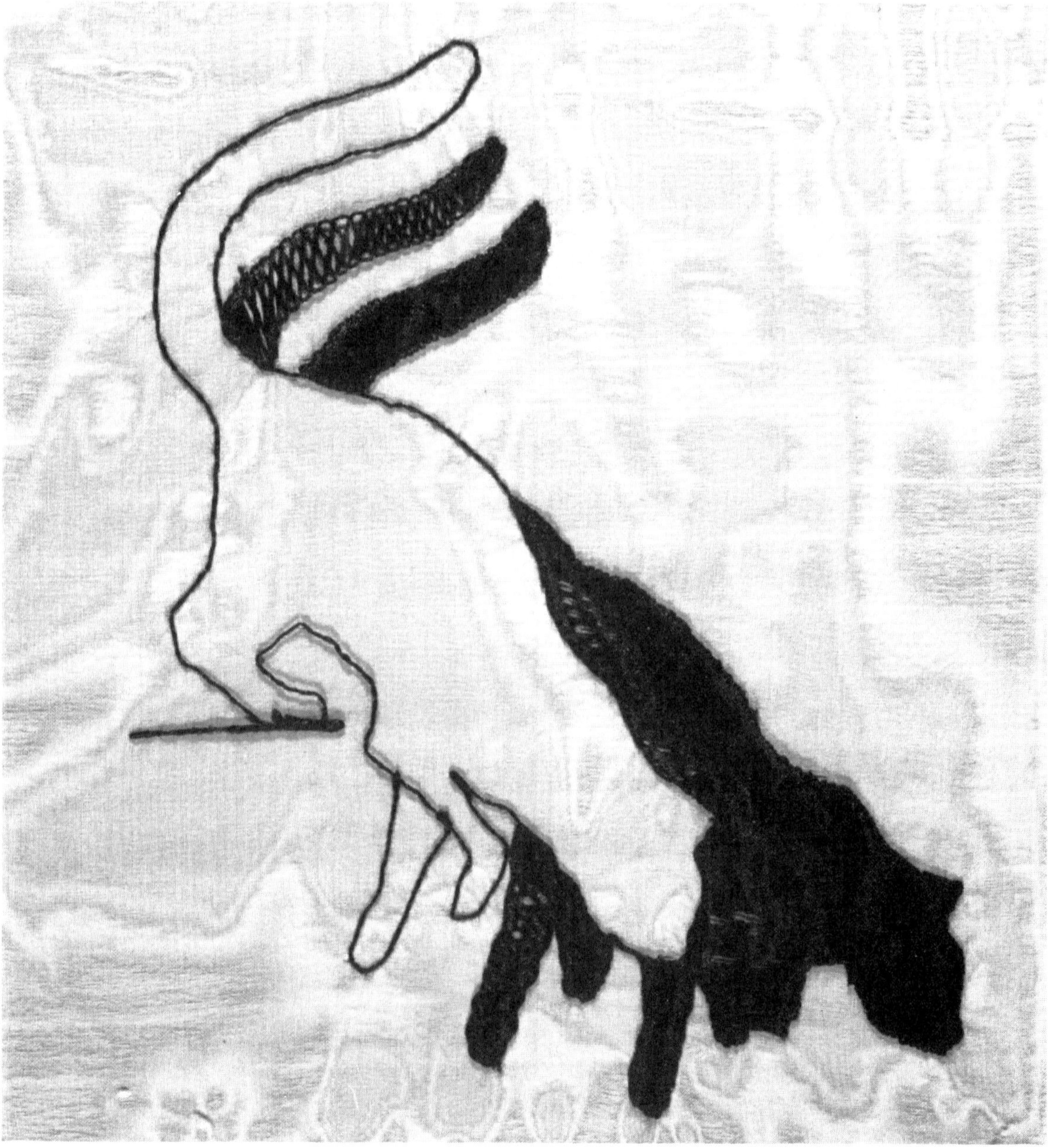

Fig. 29. *Three cats.* The darkest cat is applied black fabric. Dark fabric has been placed behind the sheer white top fabric (Frances Roche)

Fig. 28. The flower was printed onto an opaque and a sheer fabric using transfer paints. Sequins were sandwiched between the two layers and surface stitchery added (Barbara Mellor)

You will probably find it quite difficult to reproduce the exact colours at first, but the more you look, the better your sense of colour will become. As you become more confident, try to record the exact proportions of colour that you see–for instance, in a pebble coloured in many shades of grey you may see a tiny glint of pale pink, or even vivid blue. If you use that colour scheme in your embroidery, that tiny glint of bright colour will lift an otherwise quite safe scheme and make it quite exciting.

Keep all the records that you make and refer to them constantly for colour schemes for your embroidery.

Experiment with shadow work

Make some small experimental pieces using coloured fabrics and threads. Use the colour studies that you have made and collect together small quantities of coloured transparent fabrics (chiffon scarves are available in a large range of colours and are very inexpensive), coloured nets and glittery fabrics. White and pale fabrics can be coloured with fabric paints to give a lovely translucent effect.

Apply coloured fabrics behind and on the surface of the ground fabric to see what different effects can be achieved (bright red chiffon, for instance, will be very diffused when applied to the back of the fabric–the reverse when sewn to the front). Experiment with different ways of treating the edges of the fabric (see Chapter 5).

Fabrics can be bonded together using *Bondaweb* (a double-sided adhesive sheet available from haderdasher's departments). When ironing fabrics together with Bondaweb, place a sheet of baking paper over the top to prevent the iron from picking up the adhesive. The results will be much more opaque in texture than fabrics that have been applied with stitchery.

The ground fabric can be burnt away in places to reveal glittery fabrics underneath. Do not burn away too much, however, or the fabric will disintegrate!

Add surface stitchery where needed, and a few tiny, glittery beads. When you have made some experiments, work a tiny precious piece of embroidery, perhaps based on a landscape. Make your own colour scheme by using one of the suggestions in the *Colour* paragraphs.

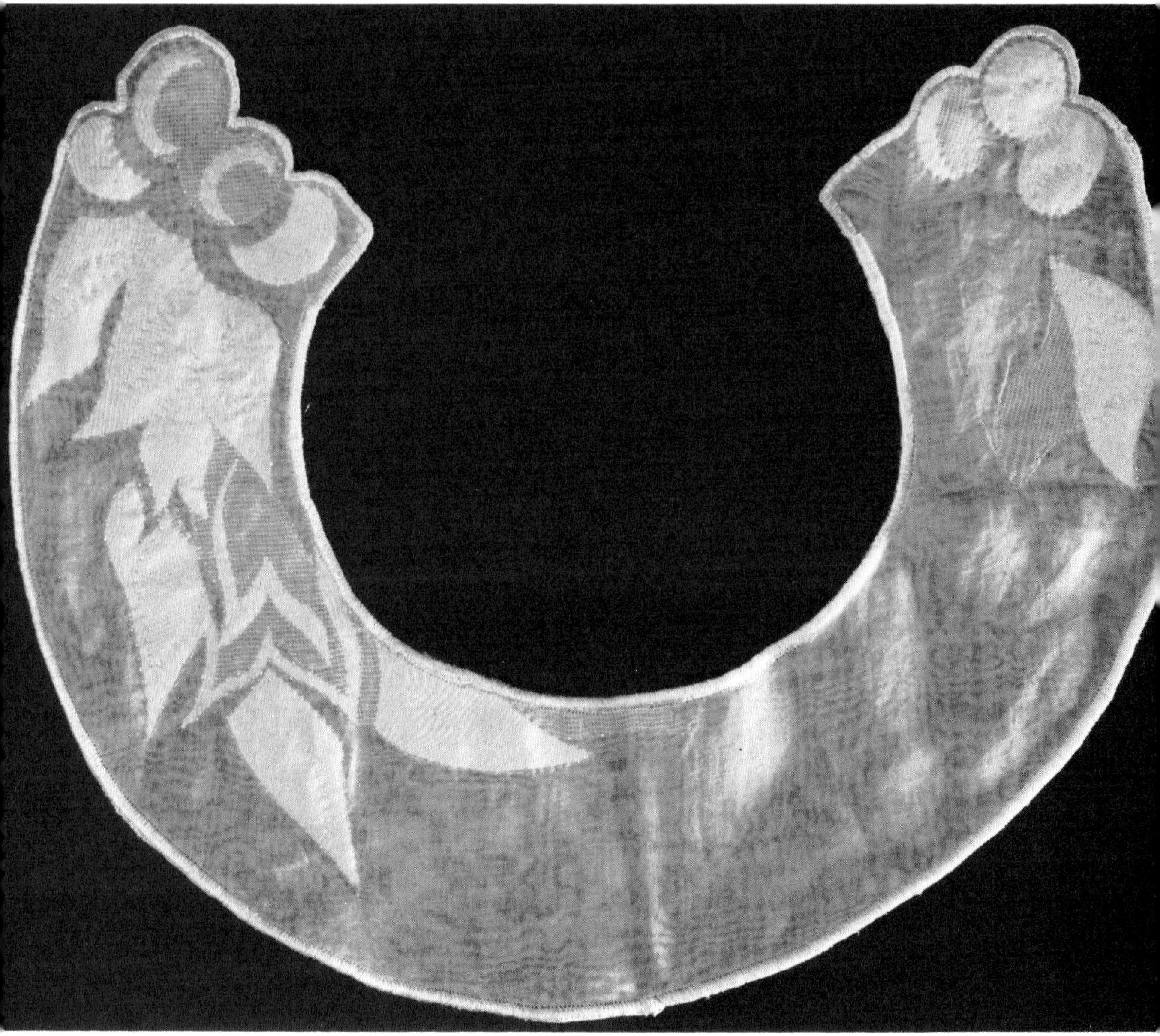

Fig. 30. Shadow work collar, the design based on drawings of celery. Net and other fabrics have been sandwiched between the two layers of organdie, and held in place with running stitches (Sarah Jowett)

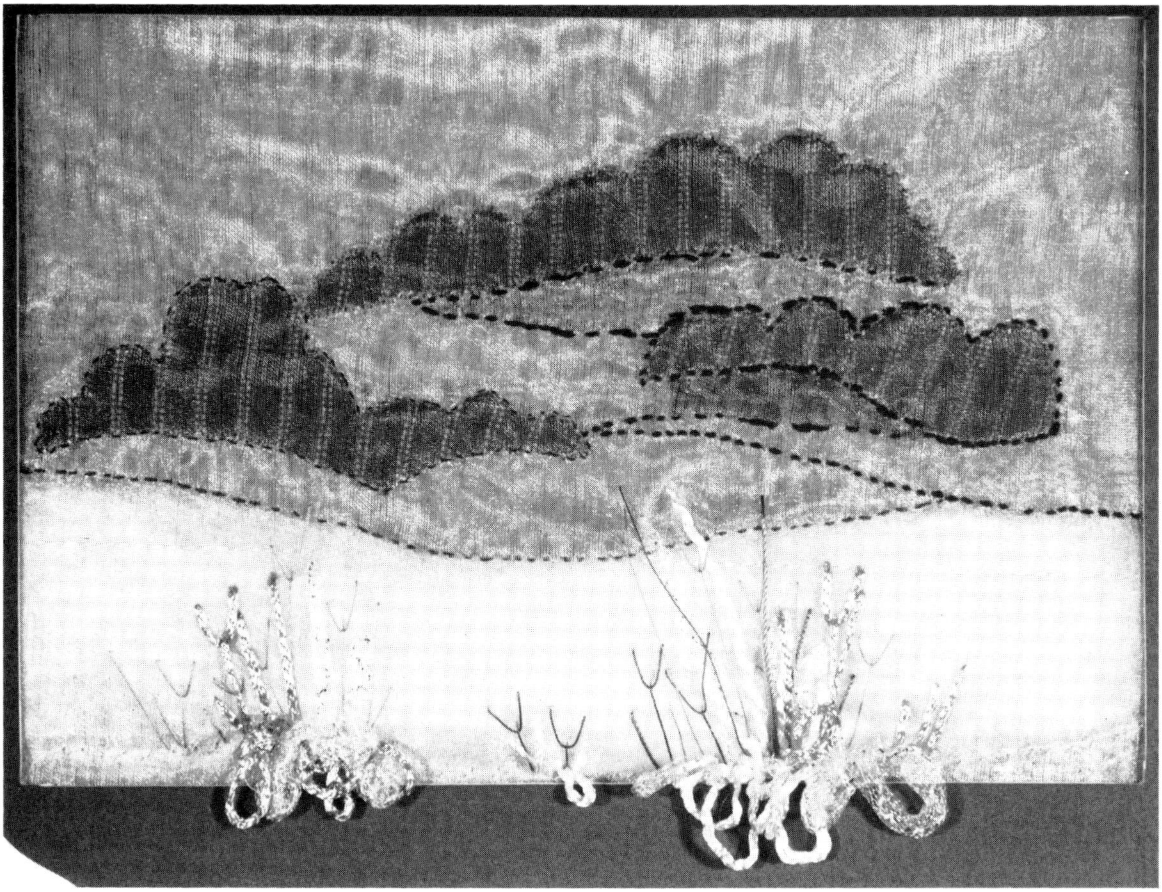

Fig. 31. Winter landscape in shadow work. Wadding and dark fabrics have been sandwiched between two layers of synthetic organza. A small amount of surface stitchery has been added to give the effect of frost on foliage (Barbara Mellor)

Four

Quilting

Quilting is arguably one of the oldest forms of embroidery. It would seem logical that it developed out of a need to make warm clothing and bedding, but there does not seem to be any substantial evidence to support this. Quilted garments were often worn as armour. Over the centuries it has been a very popular form of embroidery in England, especially for garments and bed covers. During the late nineteenth and early twentieth centuries quiltmaking flourished, particularly in the villages around Durham and in South Wales, where it became a source of additional income for miners' wives.

Fabrics and threads

Quilting is essentially a 'sandwich', usually consisting of two fabrics with a layer of wadding between.

Any smooth, slightly stretchy fabric is suitable for the top layers–e.g. silk, satin, fine cottons and synthetic fabrics. Thought must be given to the suitability of the fabric to the purpose–for instance, fabrics for a child's cot quilt should be chosen for their durability and washability.

Wadding–2oz (60g) synthetic wadding is appropriate for most quilting projects. It is washable and light enough to sew through easily.

Backing–for Trapunto and Italian quilting, butter muslin is needed. Muslin can also be used to back wadded quilting, but any fine, smooth fabric will do. Quilting wool is needed for Italian quilting.

Threads–usually the threads are of the same material as the ground fabric, i.e. silk thread for silk fabric, cotton thread for cotton. However, any thread which will slip easily through the layers of fabric is suitable. The colour of the thread is traditionally matched to that of the top fabric.

Needles should be fine and pointed–betweens are usually recommended. A large blunt needle is needed for Italian quilting. A thimble should be used, of course, and beeswax will help to prevent threads from knotting.

Transferring the design to fabric

If simple motifs are used, the easiest method is to make a template from thin card and trace around it with a sharp pointed instrument (see Chapter 1). For darker fabrics, soap makes an excellent marker. Save and dry out a sliver of soap and draw around the template with it. The soap edge can be sharpened with the blade of your scissors. This method of transferring the design is used after the fabrics have been tacked together.

For more complicated designs, the tracing and tacking method can be used. On light fabrics, the fabric can be placed on the top of the working design and traced over with a water-soluble crayon. It is probably best to avoid using water-soluble fabric markers.

Frames

With small pieces of work the quilting can be worked in the hand or in a small embroidery hoop. For larger pieces of work, quilting hoops are available or the quilting can be done on a slate frame or a large quilt frame. These last two take up a great deal of room, however. When using a hoop on large pieces of work, it is important to remember not to leave the hoop in place when you have finished quilting, as it could mark the top fabric.

Designing for quilting

Traditional quilting patterns can be adapted very successfully for modern quilting designs. Elaborate borders, such as plaited chain and feathers, could be worked in Italian or shadow quilting. Typical motifs are shells, leaves, hearts, fans, feathers and flowers, all of which are quite stylised. A row of simple hearts looks very effective on a fabric spattered with fabric paints. Any of the motifs could be used as repeat patterns to form all-over or simple border designs.

Choose a motif that is particularly appealing and use it to work through some of the following design suggestions.

1. Trace the motif on card and use the template to try out various fabric painting techniques (see Chapter 1).
2. Use the template to make repeat patterns, first as a simple spot pattern, then in a half drop repeat.
3. Use the design to make border patterns which could be particularly useful when designing for garments. Trace the designs side by side, so that the edges just touch. For the next border, overlap the motifs. Look at the new shapes produced by this method. (They are easier to see if they are coloured in.) If the design is asymmetrical, the shapes can be reversed to produce more patterns.
4. Make a printing block from the motif. If it is fairly simple, it can be cut from a potato. Use it with fabric paints to print directly on to the fabric. The designs can then be outlined with quilting stitches and other surface stitches added to give textural interest.

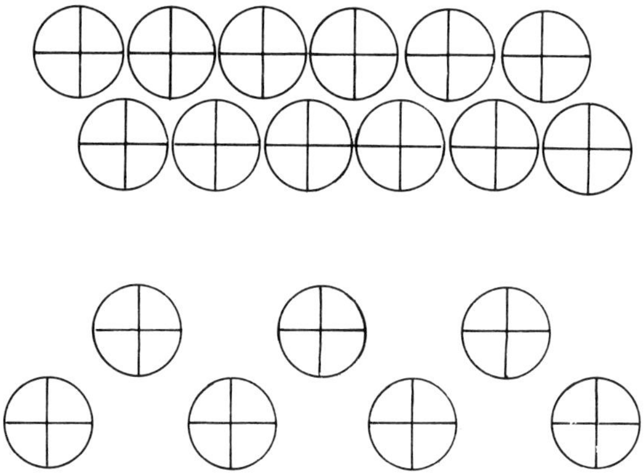

Fig. 32. Repeat patterns a) Spot pattern b) Half drop

Wadded quilting

Wadded or English quilting is the type most often used, and consists of three layers of fabric held together with stitching, usually running stitch. The three layers provide warmth and durability, making it suitable for quilts and garments.

Before any top stitching is done, the layers must be firmly tacked together, or they will slip and be very difficult to handle. Cut out the backing and wadding, making them slightly larger than the finished piece of work. Remember that quilting will 'shrink' the fabric. This is particularly important to bear in mind when making garments.

Iron the backing fabric and place on a flat surface. Smooth away any creases; the edges can be fastened to the surface with masking tape to keep the fabric in place. Place the wadding over the backing fabric. Press the top fabric and spread over the wadding.

Starting from the centre, tack the four diagonal lines, carefully smoothing the fabrics into place. Then make lines of vertical and horizontal tacking stitches so that a grid forms; the rows of tacking stitches should be approximately 3–4 inches (8–10 cm) apart. Finally, tack around the outside edge of the fabric.

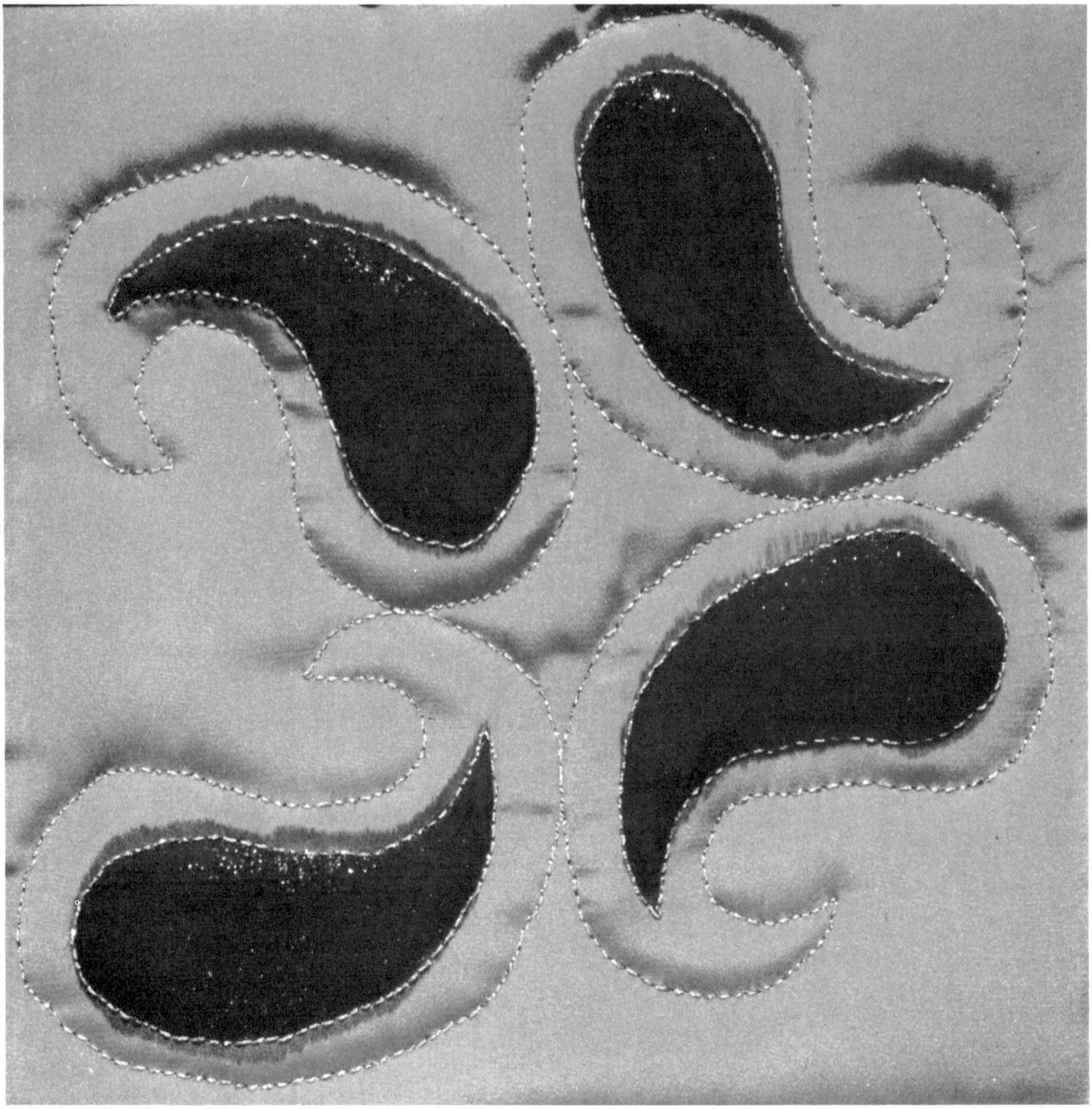

Stitches

Running stitch is most often used because it is quite fast to do and therefore suitable for large quilts and hangings. When making reversible objects (where the backing acts as the lining) it is important that the starting and finishing of stitches does not show. Wax the thread before you start and make a small knot in the end. (To prevent the thread from knotting, thread the

Fig. 33. Quilting sampler, using the paisley motif repeated several times to form a pleasing design. A stencil was used, with fabric paints, and then quilted with back stitches (Sue Pagliari)

needle from the reel before the thread is cut off.) Bring the needle through from the back of the work to the front, tugging gently until the knot disappears into the layers of fabric. To finish, bring the needle up through the last stitch, so that

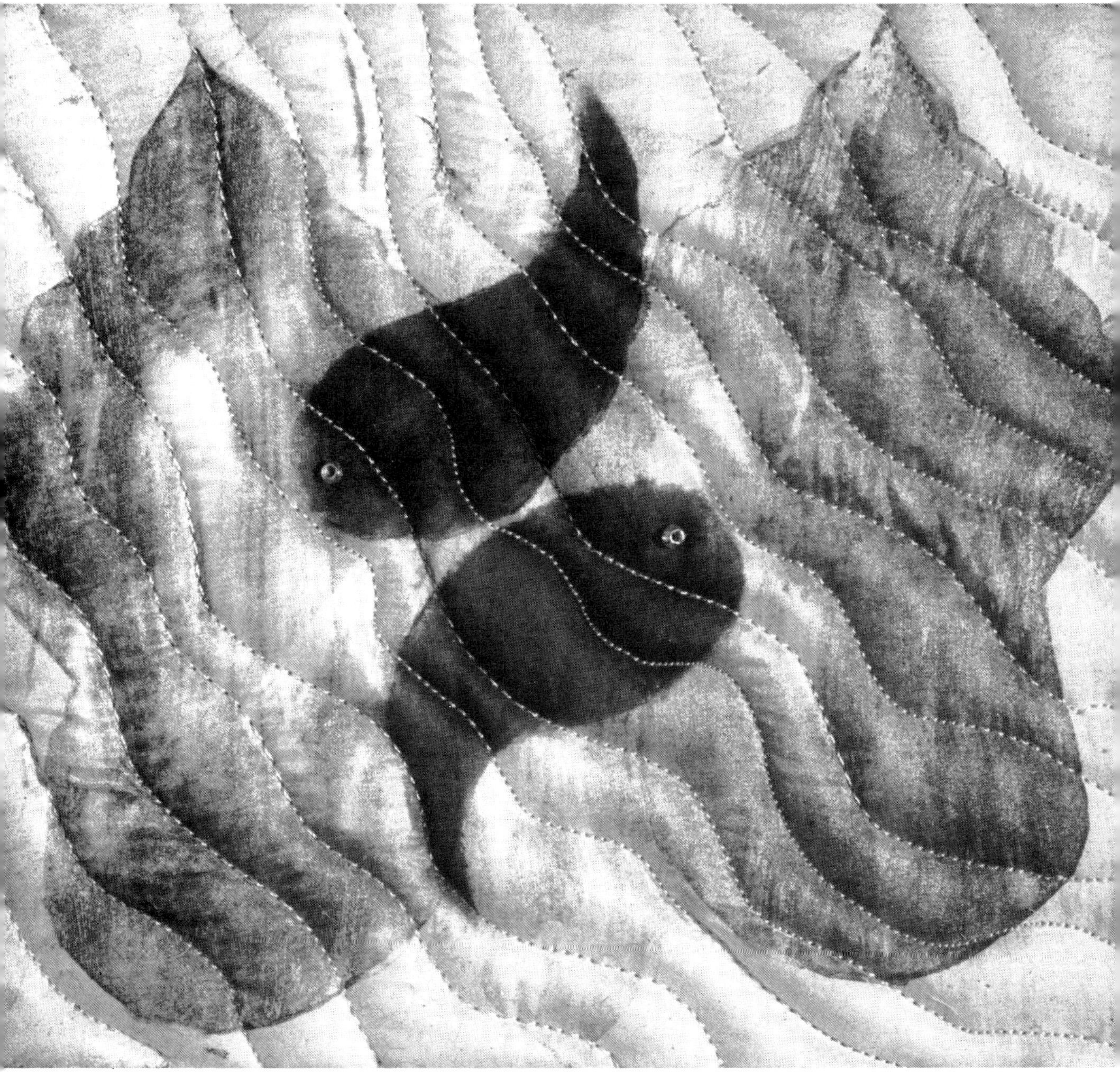

Fig. 34. The same paisley motif has been used, this time in conjunction with a thistle motif, again using a stencil and fabric paint. However, the quilting does not follow the motifs but undulates across the surface, giving the appearance of tiny fish floating in the sea (Sue Pagliari)

Fig. 35. Three layers of fabric, the top fabric, wadding and backing, are all carefully tacked together for wadded quilting

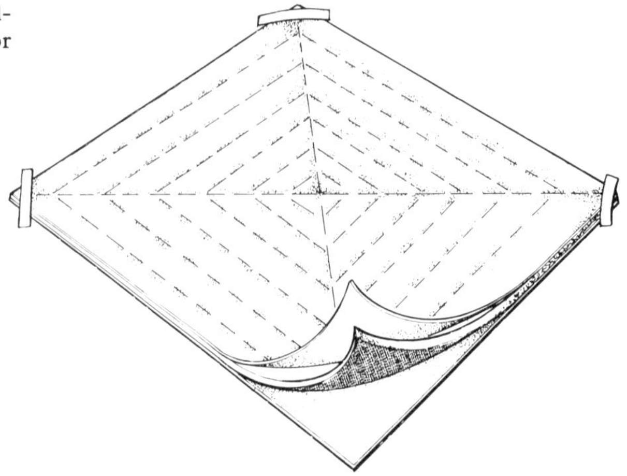

Fig. 36. The thistle motif used to produce an overlapping border pattern. Snippets of threads and fabrics have been trapped between the wadding and the transparent top fabric. The work has also been tie quilted in places (Sue Pagliari)

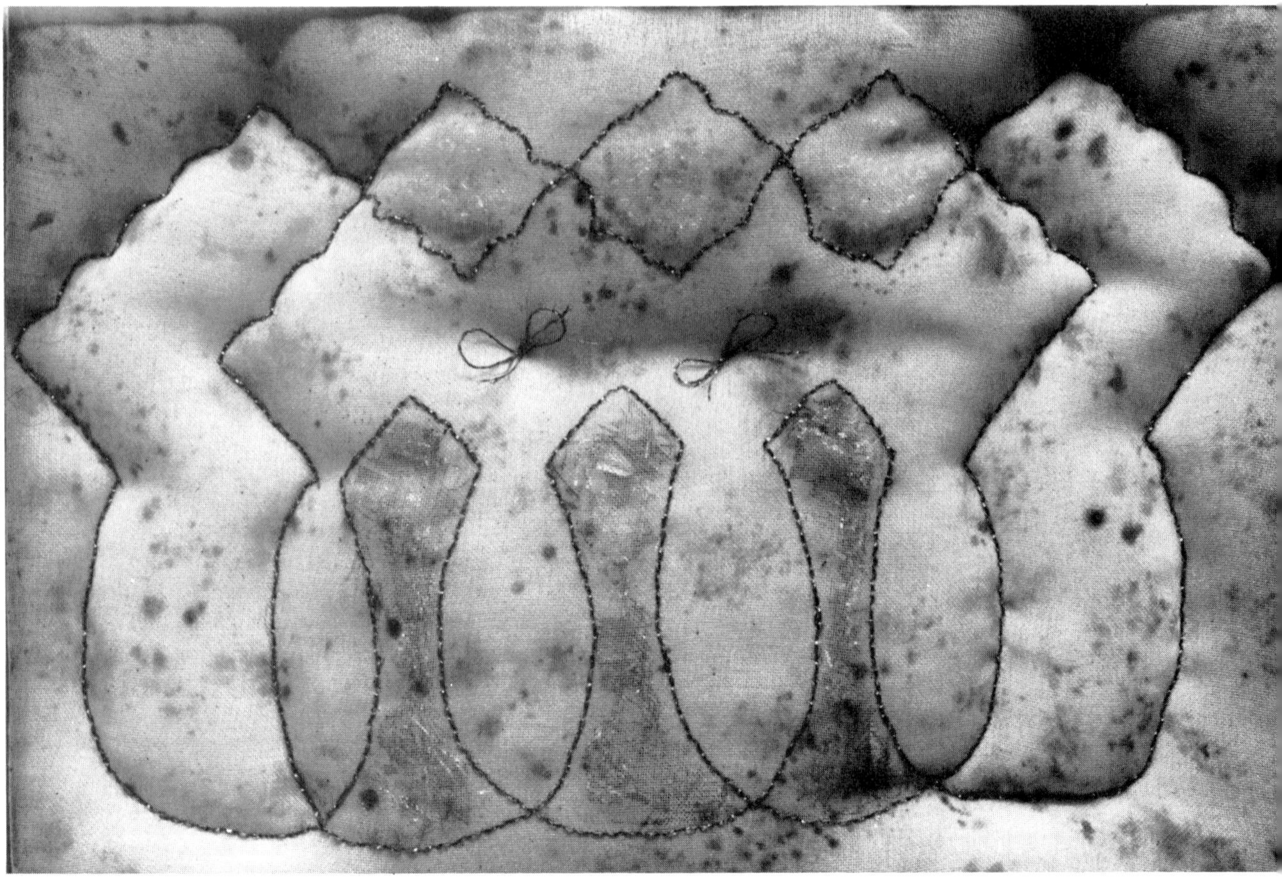

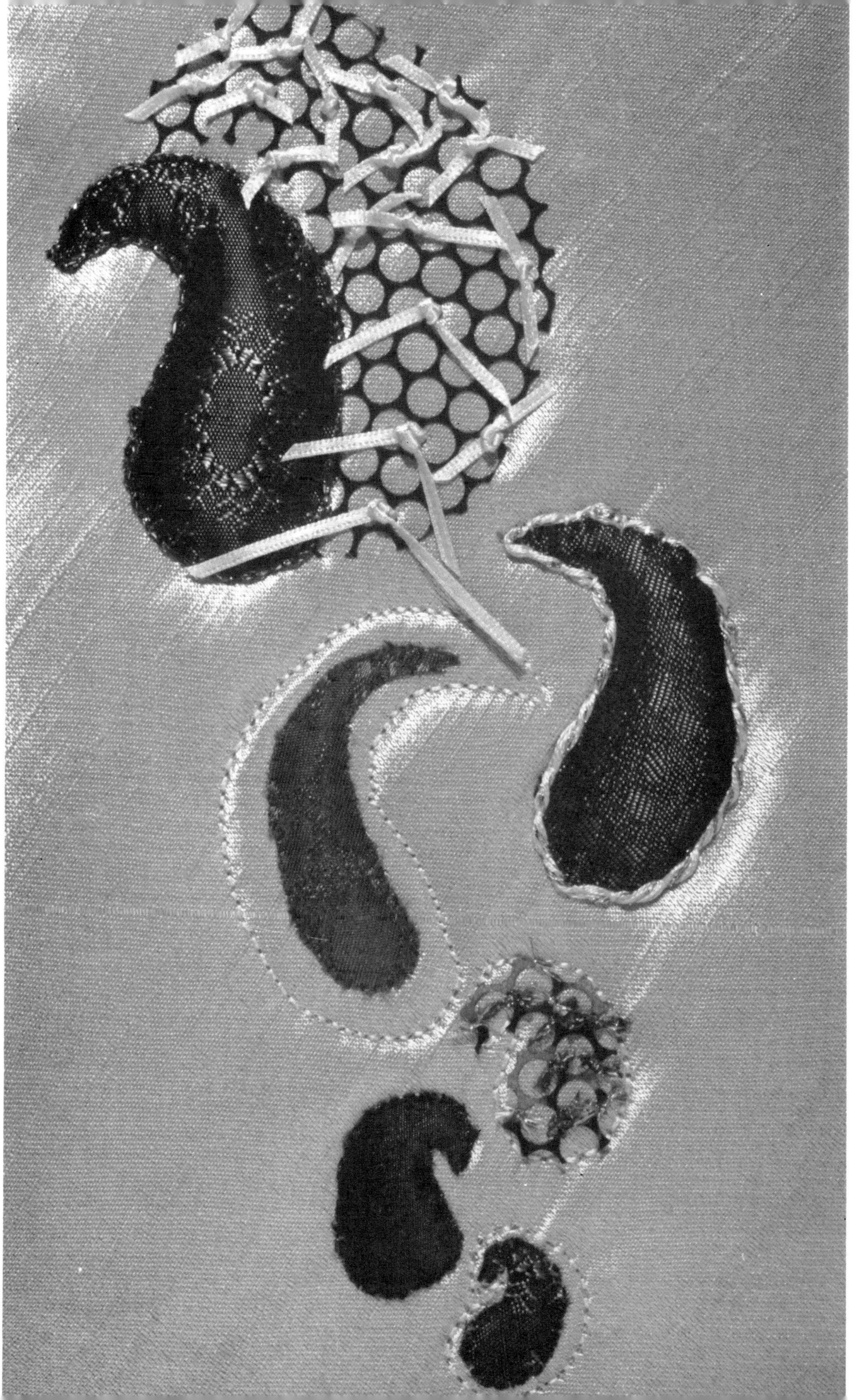

it actually pierces the thread. Pass the needle back through the top fabric only and bring it out a short distance away; trim off the surplus thread.

Begin stitching in the centre of the design and work outwards. Keep the running stitches as neat and even as possible; after a short amount of practice it will be possible to work several stitches at a time. Other linear stitches can be used successfully–e.g. back stitch, particularly when worked in a thick shiny thread, chain, stem, etc. Stitches such as seeding and french knots, together with beads and sequins, can all be used to give surface interest.

Tied quilting

Instead of using stitchery, wadded quilting can be secured by tying. This is usually worked in a formal, geometric pattern. The thread should be quite strong. The knots can be made on the top surface if desired, or on the underside if they are to be hidden away. Work one or two small stitches on the spot, leaving a thread end about $2\frac{1}{2}$ inches (6 cm) long. Cut off the working thread and tie the ends together with a slip knot. Trim off the ends of the threads to about 2 cm–if they are any shorter than this they will soon become unravelled. Beads, buttons or french knots could be substituted successfully for knots.

Trapunto

Trapunto, or stuffed quilting, is a more decorative type of quilting as only certain areas of the design are padded, after the stitchery is worked.

The backing fabric should be loosely woven–butter muslin is ideal for this. Prepare the fabrics as for wadded quilting, but omit the wadding.

The design should be transferred to the fabric before tacking together. When designing for this type of quilting, it is important to remember that the shapes to be padded must be entirely enclosed with stitchery. Back stitch is generally used for trapunto quilting.

Fig. 37. The paisley design has been used again, but this time by a different embroiderer. Fabrics have been applied to the surface and trapunto quilted. Sequin waste has been cut into shapes and applied and parts of the design have been tie quilted with narrow ribbon (Karyl Cragg)

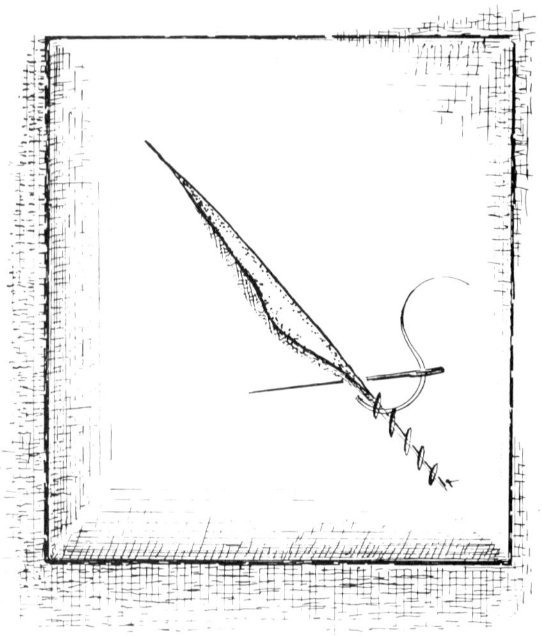

Fig. 38. Trapunto. Make a small slit in the back of the muslin to insert the filling. Oversew the slit when filled

After all the stitchery has been worked, the design can be padded. Make a small slit in the muslin with sharp embroidery scissors, being very careful not to cut the top fabric as well. Tease out a little wadding or cotton wool and insert into the shape with a fine crochet hook. When the space is filled, sew up the slit in the middle with a few overcasting stitches.

Italian quilting

Like Trapunto, Italian or 'corded' quilting is purely decorative and consists of a cord inserted between two lines of parallel stitching. Flowing designs and interlaced patterns are all particularly suitable. Quilting wool can be purchased at embroidery shops–it is thick, loosly spun and cream-coloured.

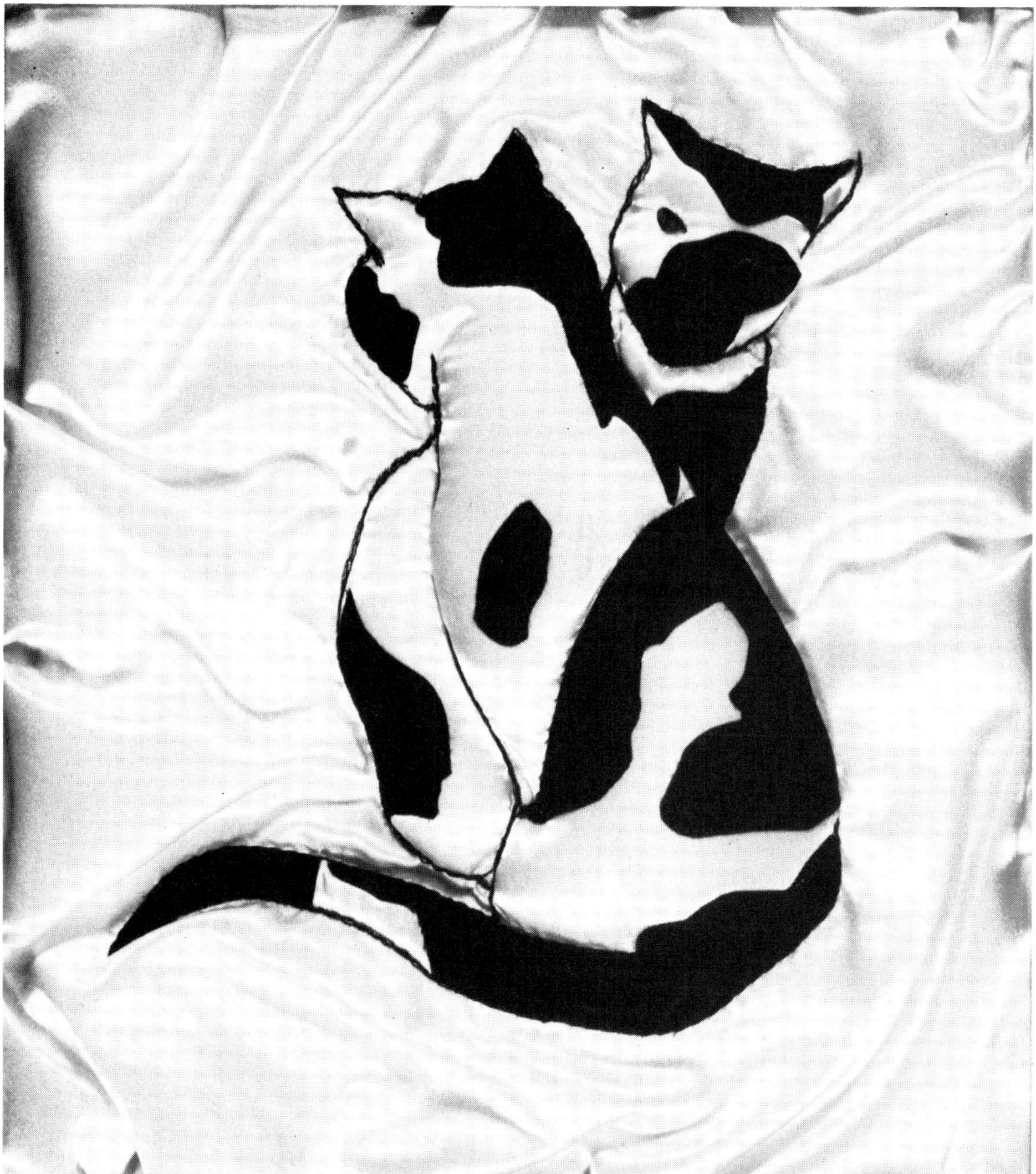

Fig. 39. Two cats in Trapunto quilting. The black patches have been applied with Bondaweb. The cats are very raised, and the satin background has been ruched, to give a luxurious feel (Frances Roche)

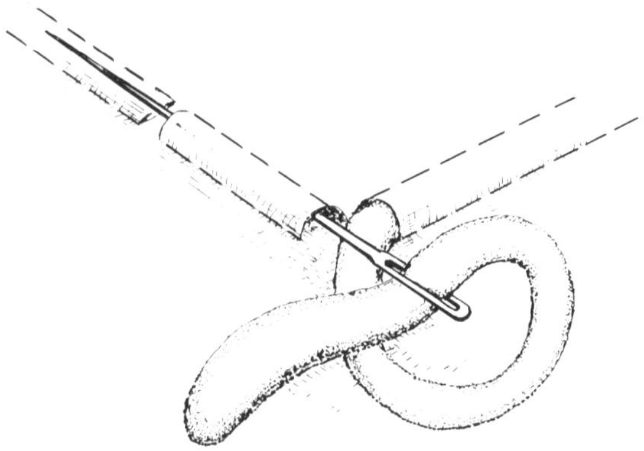

Fig. 40. Italian quilting. On the wrong side of the work thread the quilting wool through the two rows of stitching. Leave a small loop of wool at the corners.

Fig. 41. *The Box Room,* a miniature fabric house. Parts of the design, including the stylised tree, have been worked in Italian quilting. The roof is also wadded quilted and the sides flat quilted. The box opens up to reveal a miniature room complete with furnishings including a bed with a patchwork quilt (Cynthia Sherwood)

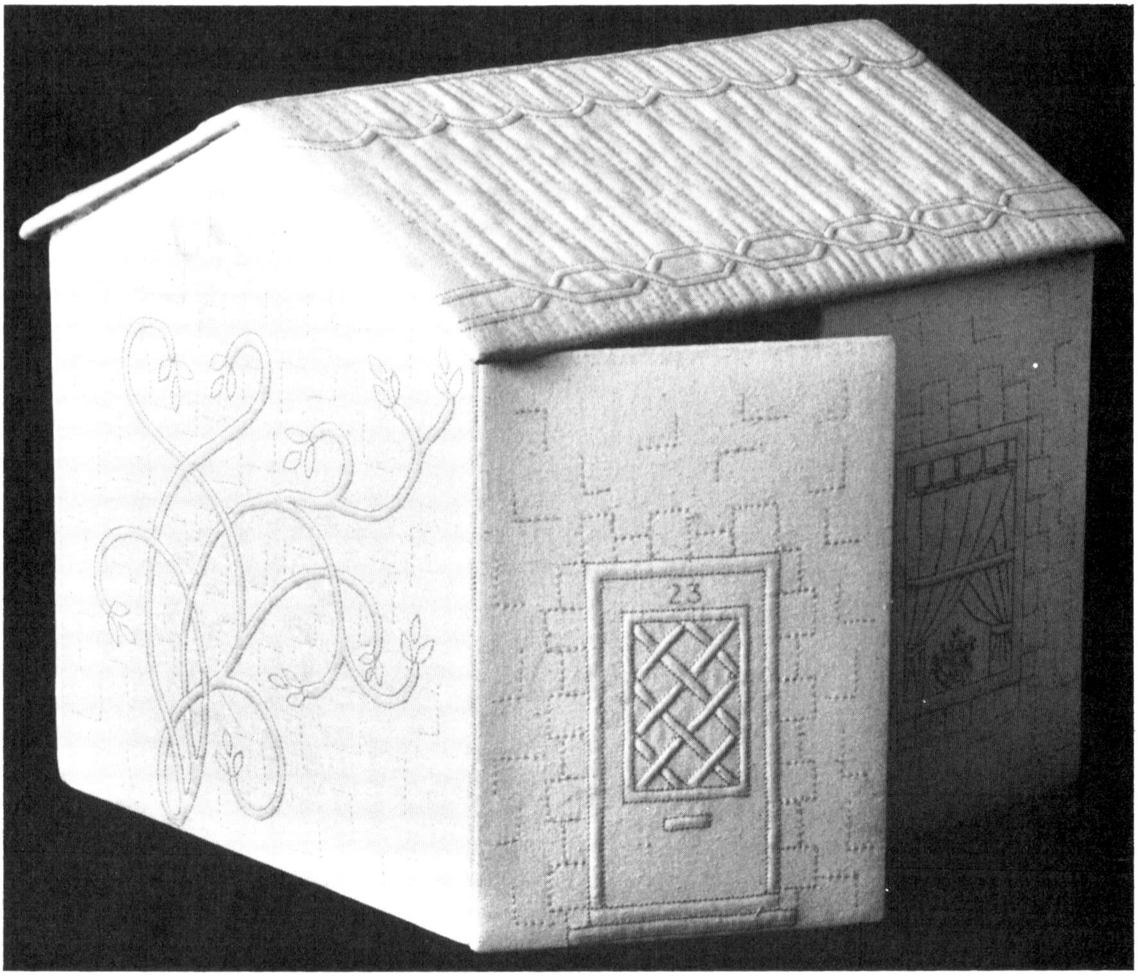

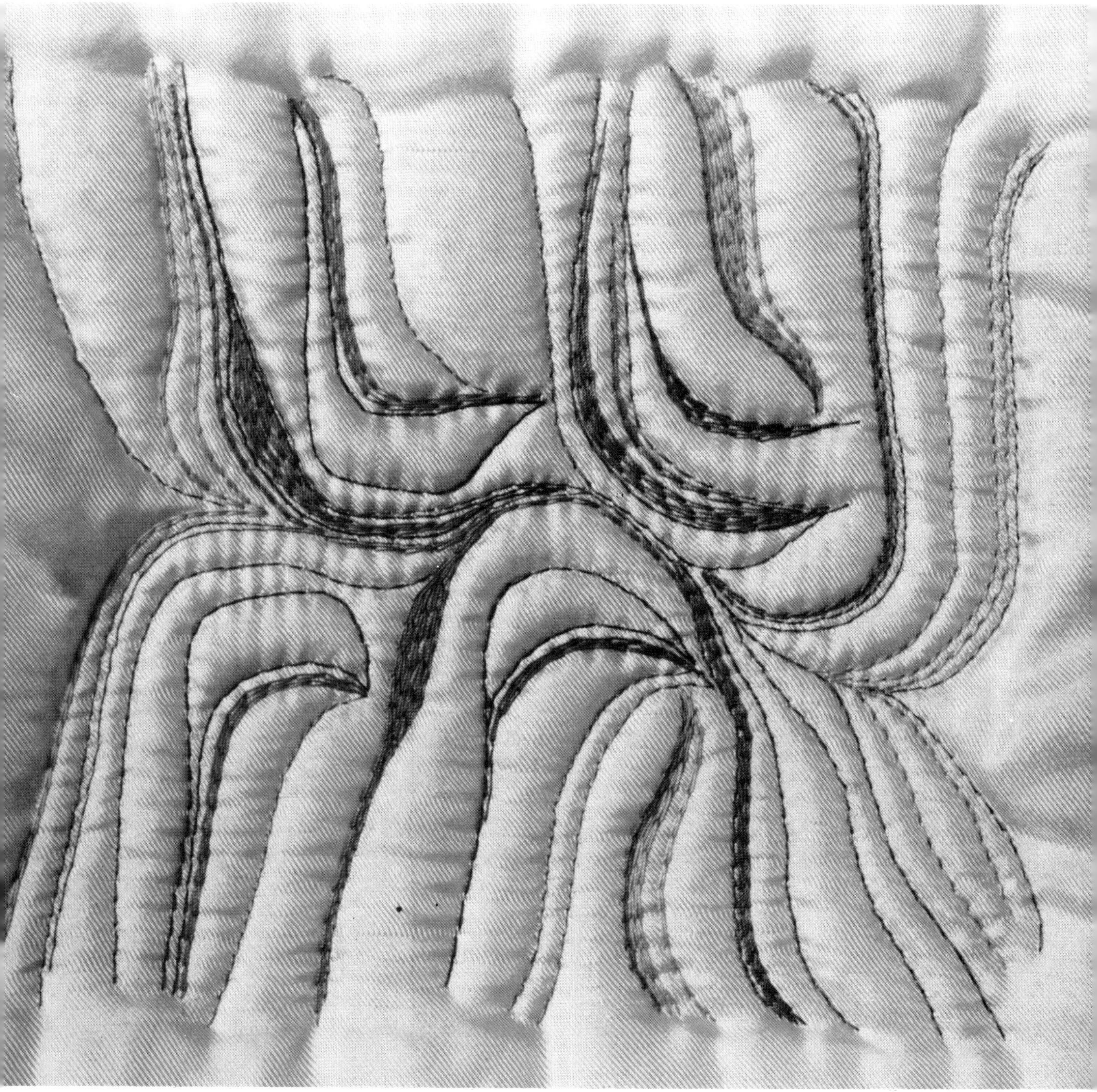

Fig. 42. Sampler of wadding quilting using different coloured threads and a combination of stitches including back and chain stitch (Muriel Best)

Transfer the design to the top fabric and tack the fabric to a piece of muslin. Work the design using back stitch. (The rows of stitchery could equally well be worked on a sewing machine using a straight stitch.)

When the stitching has been completed, turn the work to the wrong side. Thread a length of quilting wool into a large-eyed blunt needle. Insert the needle through the backing fabric only, making sure that it does not pierce the top fabric. Take the needle along the row of stitching taking care not to pull or pucker the fabrics. When a corner is reached, the needle should be pulled out of the muslin and reinserted in the same spot, leaving a small loop on the surface. If a fine, pale fabric is used, a vividly coloured knitting wool could be substituted for the quilting wool and will give a slight hint of colour to the quilting.

Surface stitchery can be added to both trapunto and Italian quilting after they have been quilted.

Both types of work will need to be relined after working, as the butter muslin will not give adequate protection. Both methods can successfully be used with wadded quilting to give added definition and extra warmth to a particular piece of work. In either method the stitching and padding should be worked first and all tacking threads removed. The fabric is then tacked to the wadding and lining fabric and quilted through all the layers.

Shadow quilting

Shadow quilting usually follows the trapunto or Italian quilting methods. The top fabric is sheer, e.g. organdie, chiffon or organza, and the backing is usually a firm cotton, although two layers of sheer fabric can be sandwiched together. The fillings should be of very bright, clear colours as they will appear very muted when worked. Bright wools and cords or braids can be used for corded quilting.

For larger areas, as in trapunto, threads can be chopped into small lengths and inserted into the shapes through a slit made in the backing. Brightly coloured fabrics can also be used, including felts, lurex and silks. These should all be chopped into tiny pieces. Beads and sequins can also be used as stuffing.

After the stuffing has been worked, any surface stitchery can be added.

Methods of finishing for all types of quilting can be found in Chapter 8.

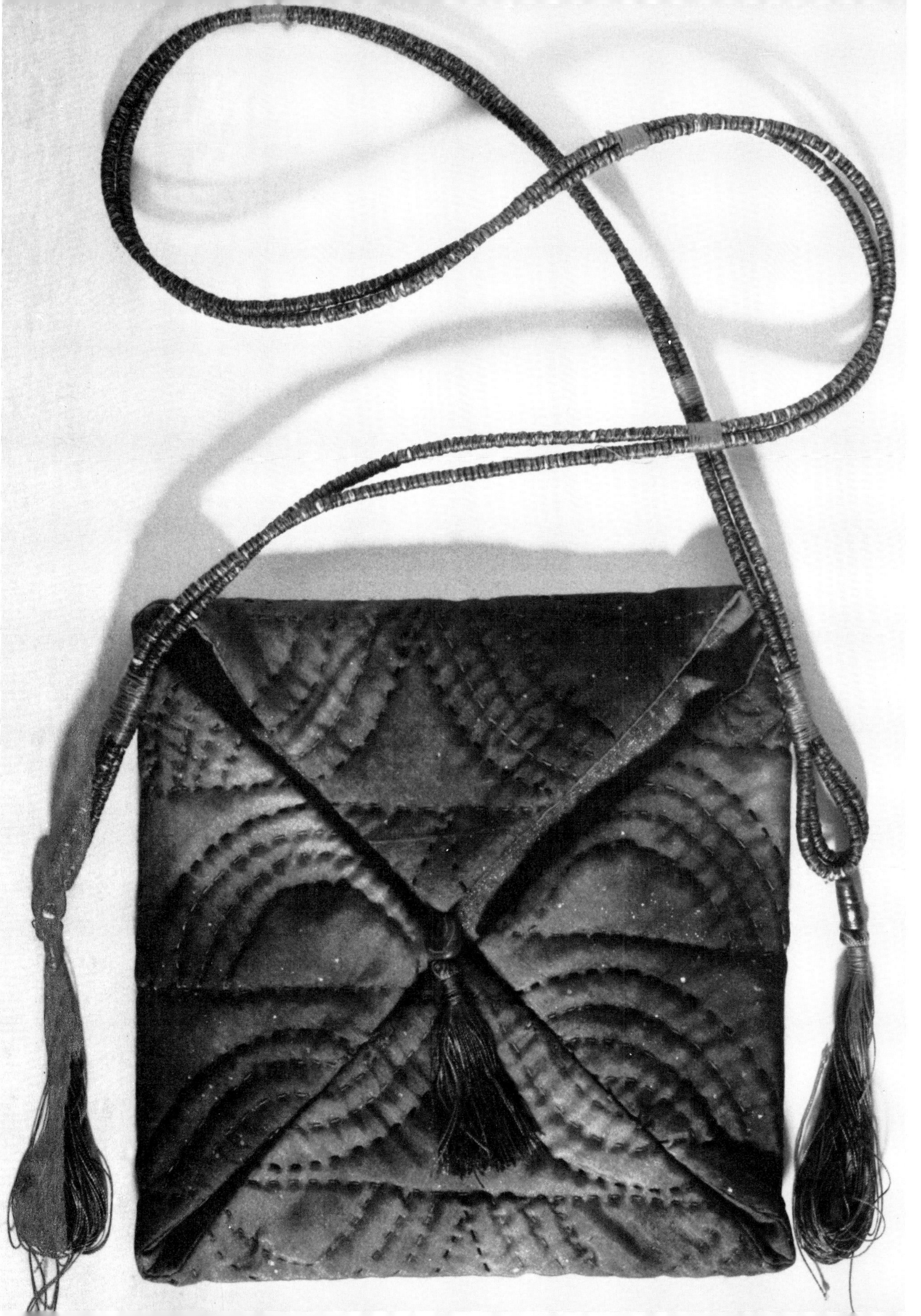

Five

Appliqué

An ancient form of needlework, appliqué, or applied work, today exists in many styles and techniques, throughout the world. Since the eighteenth century it has been used extensively in Britain and the United States, on quilts and bedcovers, sometimes combined with patchwork, and often quilted. The Kuna Indians of the San Blas Islands make *molas*, which are layers of brightly coloured, plain fabrics with areas cut away to reveal the colours beneath. In India large hangings are made, usually using simple, geometric shapes in bright colours, and in Africa, leather is used to decorate hangings and garments.

Fabrics

Almost any fabric can be used for appliqué. The main consideration is suitability for finished purpose. For garments, quilts and other objects that need to be washed frequently, cottons and polyester cottons are most suitable. For items that are intended to be purely decorative, fabrics such as velvets, fine silks, lace, leathers and organzas can all be used. For fabrics that are likely to fray, Bondaweb can be used to stick the fabric to the background. Felt is very easy to work with, as it will not fray, but it is not washable and fades if hung in bright sunlight for very long.

Fig. 43. A small envelope bag, using a border pattern as design (Jenny Bullen)

The sewing thread should, if possible, match the fabric, i.e. silk to silk, cotton to cotton etc. Its colour should, if possible, closely match the shapes to be applied.

Fine sewing needles, betweens or crewels, and fine, rustless pins for securing patches are especially important.

Frames

This will be very much a matter for the individual. If you are using fabrics that are difficult to handle, it will probably be easier to use a frame.

Transfering designs to fabric

If using simple, uncomplicated shapes, the easiest method is to trace the design on stiff paper and use this as a cutting guide.

Hand-stitched appliqué

To begin, it is probably best to choose a very simple shape and fabrics that are easy to handle, such as pure cotton, which will crease beautifully. New cottons should always be washed before use, to remove any dressing and excess colour.

Carefully press all the fabrics. Lay the ground fabric on a flat surface, or use a small frame if preferred.

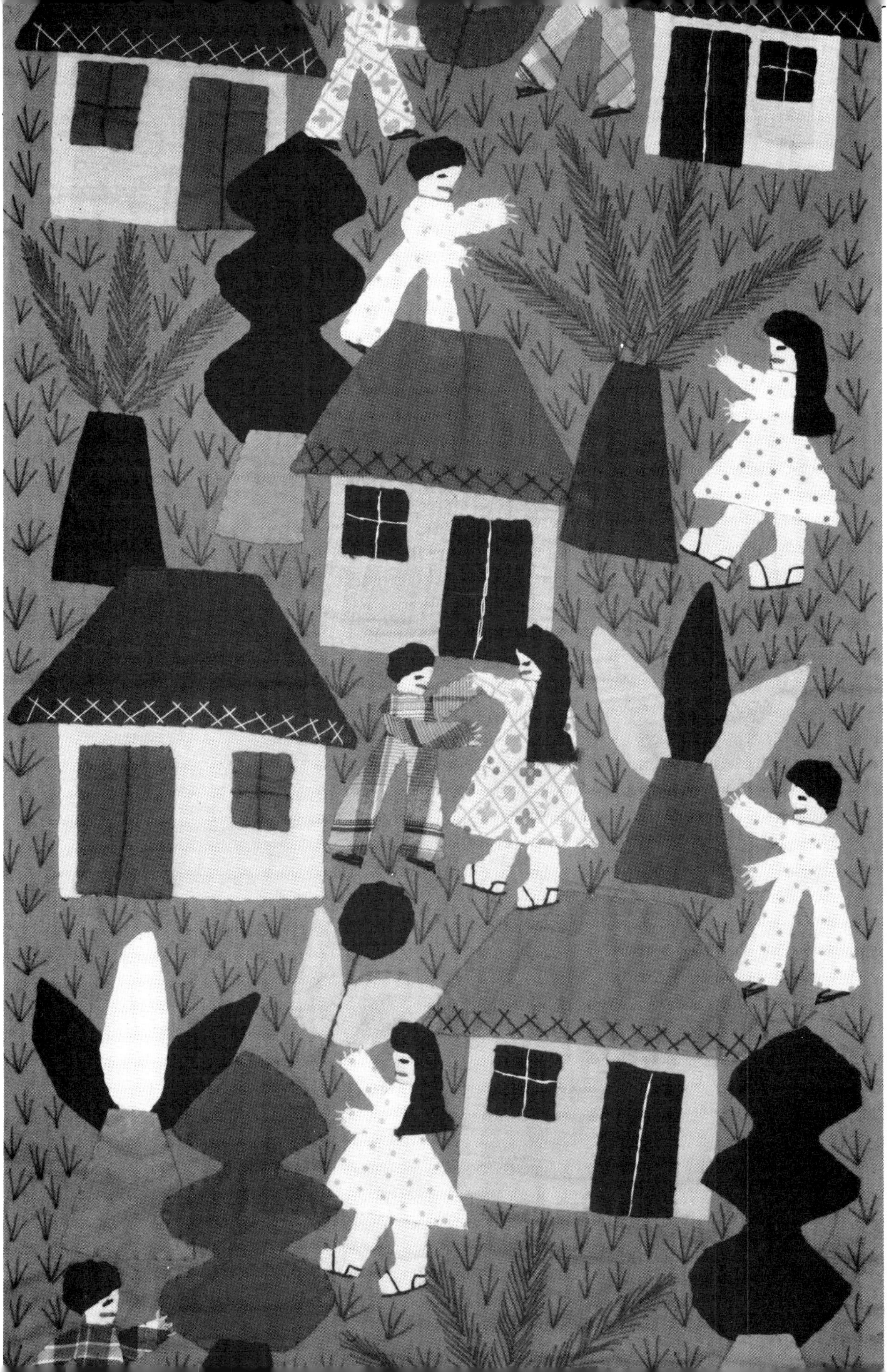

Transfer the design to stiff paper and cut out the templates. Pin the template on to the fabric. Draw carefully around the shape (a hard pencil will do for this). Carefully cut $\frac{1}{4}$ inch (6 mm) from the drawn line, to provide the seam allowance. Using small, sharp embroidery scissors, clip into all corners or curves, being careful not to cut the fabric beyond the drawn line. Turn under, press and tack all the seam allowances. Pin the applied shapes to the background fabric. If the shapes are complicated or very large, they should then be tacked into place. Then, using a matching thread, slip stitch all around carefully. Remove all the tacking threads and press the fabrics. Surface embroidery stitches can be added at this stage, if required, or the work could be quilted to add an extra dimension.

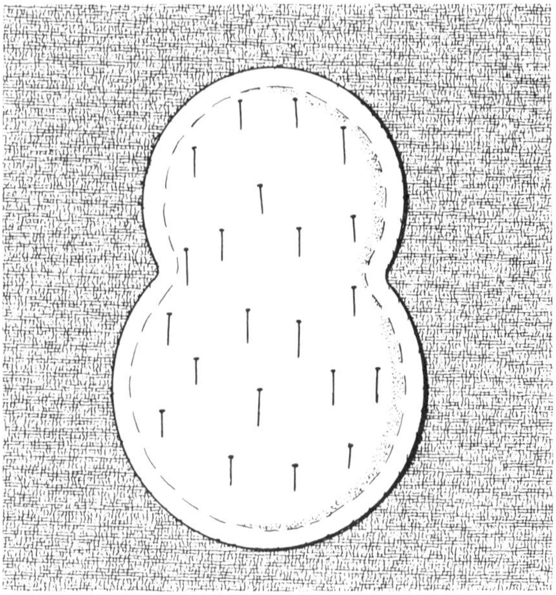

Fig. 45. Applied shapes should be pinned to the background fabric, matching the grain lines of both fabrics if possible. If the shapes are very complicated, they should be tacked in place before being hem stitched

Machine appliqué

Applying fabrics using the zigzag stitch on a sewing machine is a great deal quicker than sewing by hand and gives quite hard-wearing results. Choose a good-quality sewing thread, preferably in a colour to match the applied shapes.

Prepare the fabrics as for hand stitching. Cut out the shapes, but do not include any seam allowances, pin and tack to the background fabric. If fabrics are liable to fray or are particularly fine, secure them with Bondaweb. Iron the Bondaweb to the fabric and then trace around the templates on the right side. Cut out the shapes, peel away the protective paper and place them on the fabric. Press into place, remembering to put a sheet of baking parchment on top of the fabrics to prevent the iron from sticking.

Using a fairly close zigzag and a medium-length stitch, carefully stitch around all the applied shapes. Leave loose ends of threads at the beginning and ending of each row rather than using reverse stitch to neaten. When all the shapes have been sewn down, thread the loose ends to the

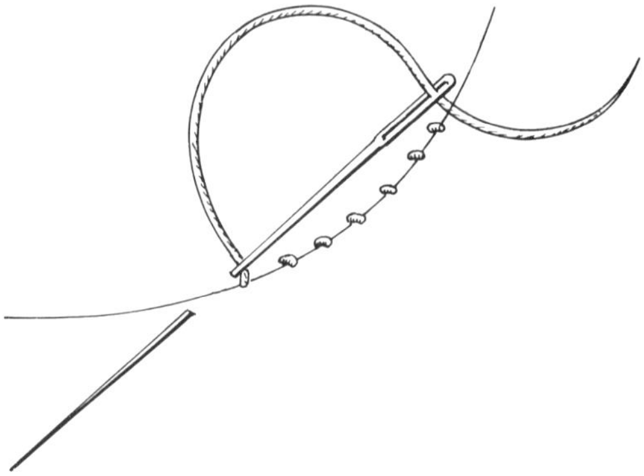

Fig. 46. Hem stitch. The thread should match the colour of the fabric, and the stitches be as small and as neat as possible

Fig. 44. Section of a Mexican embroidered wall hanging. Houses, figures and trees, in brightly coloured cottons, have all been applied by hand, with added embroidery stitches (by courtesy of Diana Mitchell)

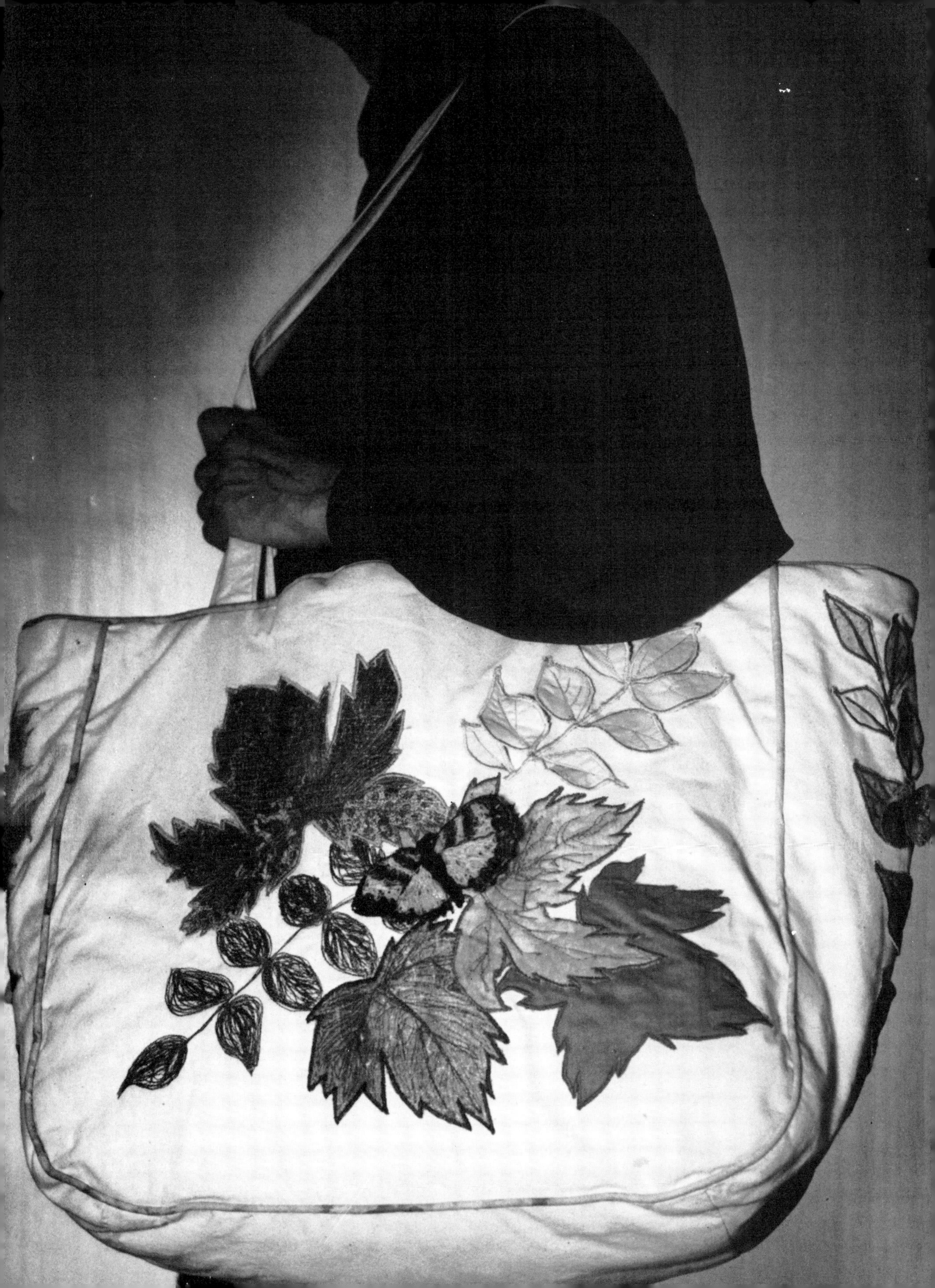

wrong side of the work and secure them by hand. Machine stitch is very easy to do, but does require a little practice, and so it is advisable to make a sample before attempting a finished piece of work.

Both of the methods described above are very hard-wearing and therefore suitable for items such as quilts and cushions, which will take a lot of wear and tear. However, for purely decorative effects, such as in an embroidered picture, more unusual fabrics can be used and suggestions are given below of ways of treating the edges and attaching them to the background fabric.

1. Frayed edges can look very attractive and add a great deal of interest to a piece of embroidery. Most woven fabrics will fray. They should be attached to the background fabric with tiny stab stitches in a matching thread.
2. Fabric can be burnt along the edges. Natural fibres are best for this, but you can experiment with man-made fabrics. Most of these will give off toxic fumes, so make sure that you work in a well-ventilated room. Hold the fabric over a candle flame and work near a bowl of water.
3. Sheer fabrics and nets can be used to great effect, particularly when different colours are laid over each other. The edges can be frayed or burnt, or simply attached to the background with tiny herringbone stitches, or stab stitch.
4. The edges of the fabric can be trimmed with pinking shears. This works best if the fabric is cut on the bias, as it tends to fray less.
5. Felt can be sewn down with tiny stab stitches close to the edge; care should be taken not to handle the edges too much as they have a tendency to stretch. Leather can be treated in the same way. Soft gloving leathers and suedes can usually be sewn with a fine sewing needle, but tougher qualities will require a gloving needle, which has a triangular point.

Fig. 47. 'Countryside' bag in calico, with leaves and insects applied by machine. Some of the insects and leaves are three-dimensional (Chris Wilkins)

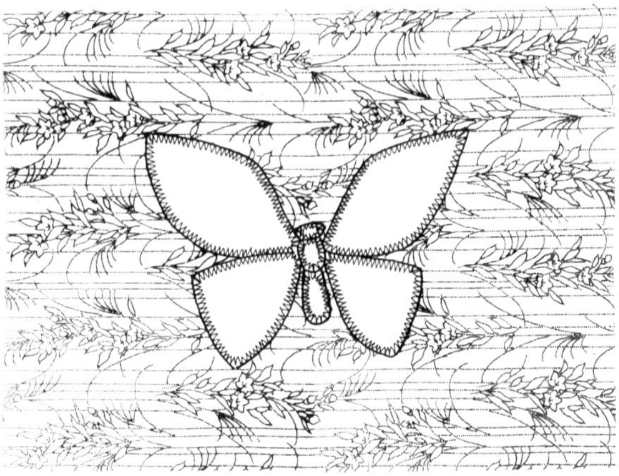

Fig. 48. Machine appliqué, using a close zigzag stitch

Design for appliqué

Buildings and architectural features of all kinds are excellent starting points when designing for appliqué. Houses can be treated in a naturalistic way with detail added in surface embroidery, or be purely abstract so that the original design is almost lost in the finished work.

It is a good idea to start a sketchbook. Collect photographs and magazine cuttings, and, most important, draw. Use quick sketches, a few lines to depict anything of interest to you–houses, shops, barns, market stalls or seaside piers. Doors and windows are excellent for embroidery; windows can be depicted opening on to beautiful gardens or busy streets; doors can show tantalising glimpses of courtyards beyond. Other suggestions are roofs and chimneys, brickwork, modern glass buildings, ruins of old houses, castles, etc.

Cut paper designs are a good way of bridging the gap between design and interpretation into fabric. Select a simple shape, perhaps an interesting window, and cut it out several times in tissue paper. Overlap the shapes to make an interesting border pattern. Where the papers overlap, new shapes and patterns will emerge. This sort of design could be worked very successfully in sheer fabrics.

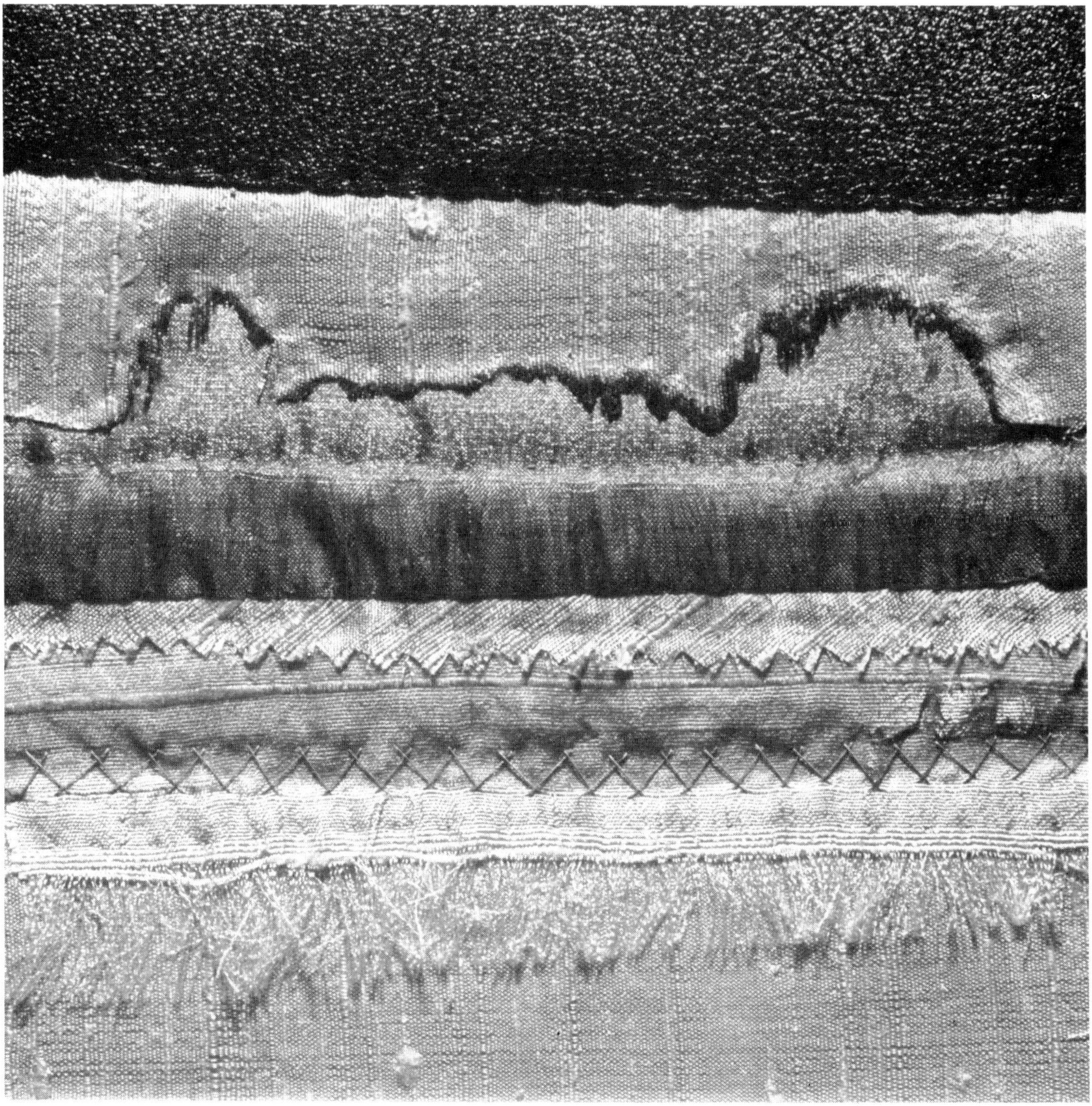

Fig. 49. Methods of treating edges of fabric for appliqué. From the top: a) leather applied with stab stitch b) a burnt edge c) frayed organza d) edge of fabric turned under and hem stitched in place e) pinked edge on the diagonal of the fabric f) herringbone stitch used to hold fabric in place g) frayed silk

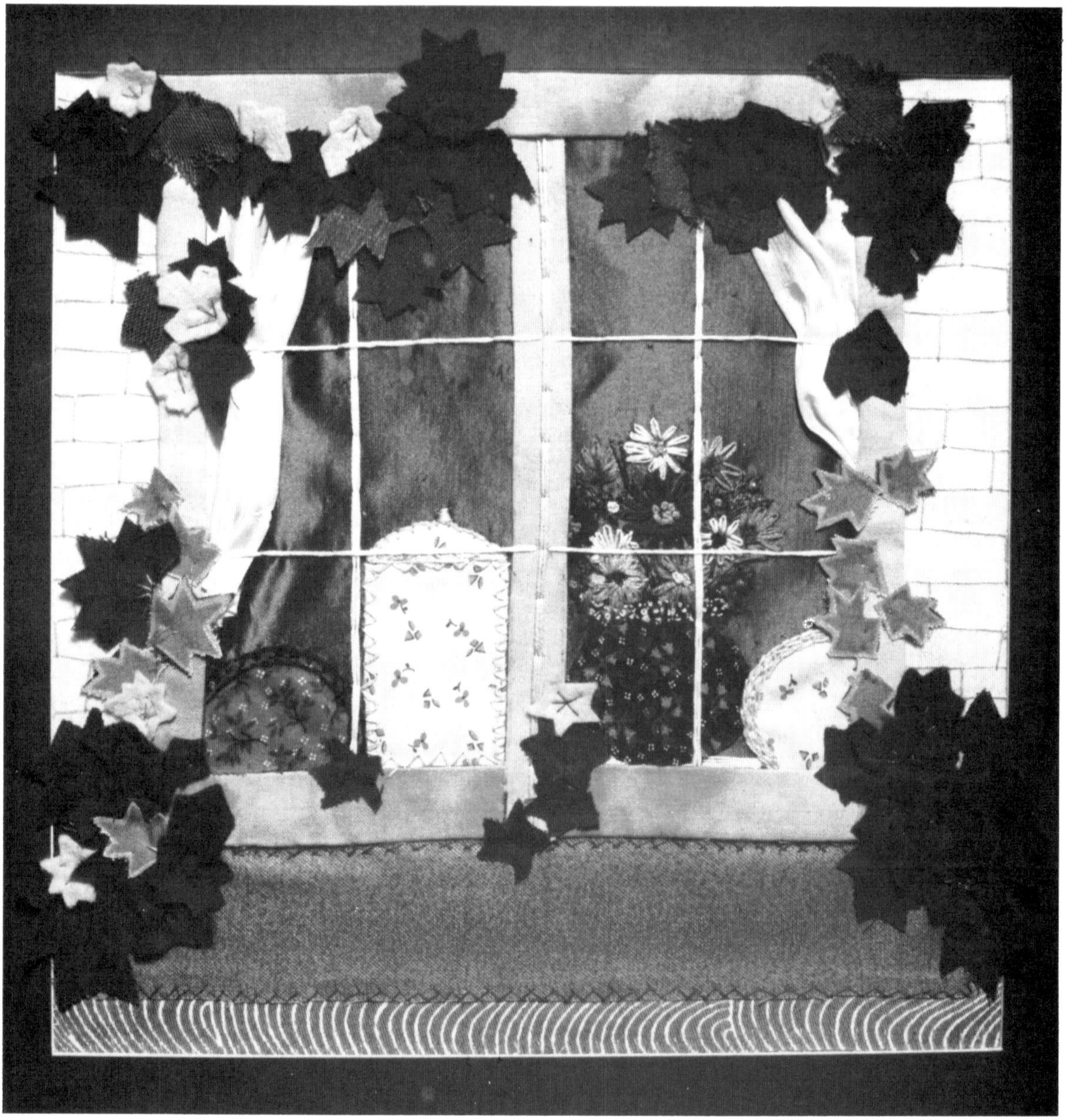

Fig. 50. A variety of different fabrics have been used to create this small panel showing a window with glimpses of the room inside. Tiny leaf shapes have been cut out and applied by hand to surround the window (Tracey Maquire)

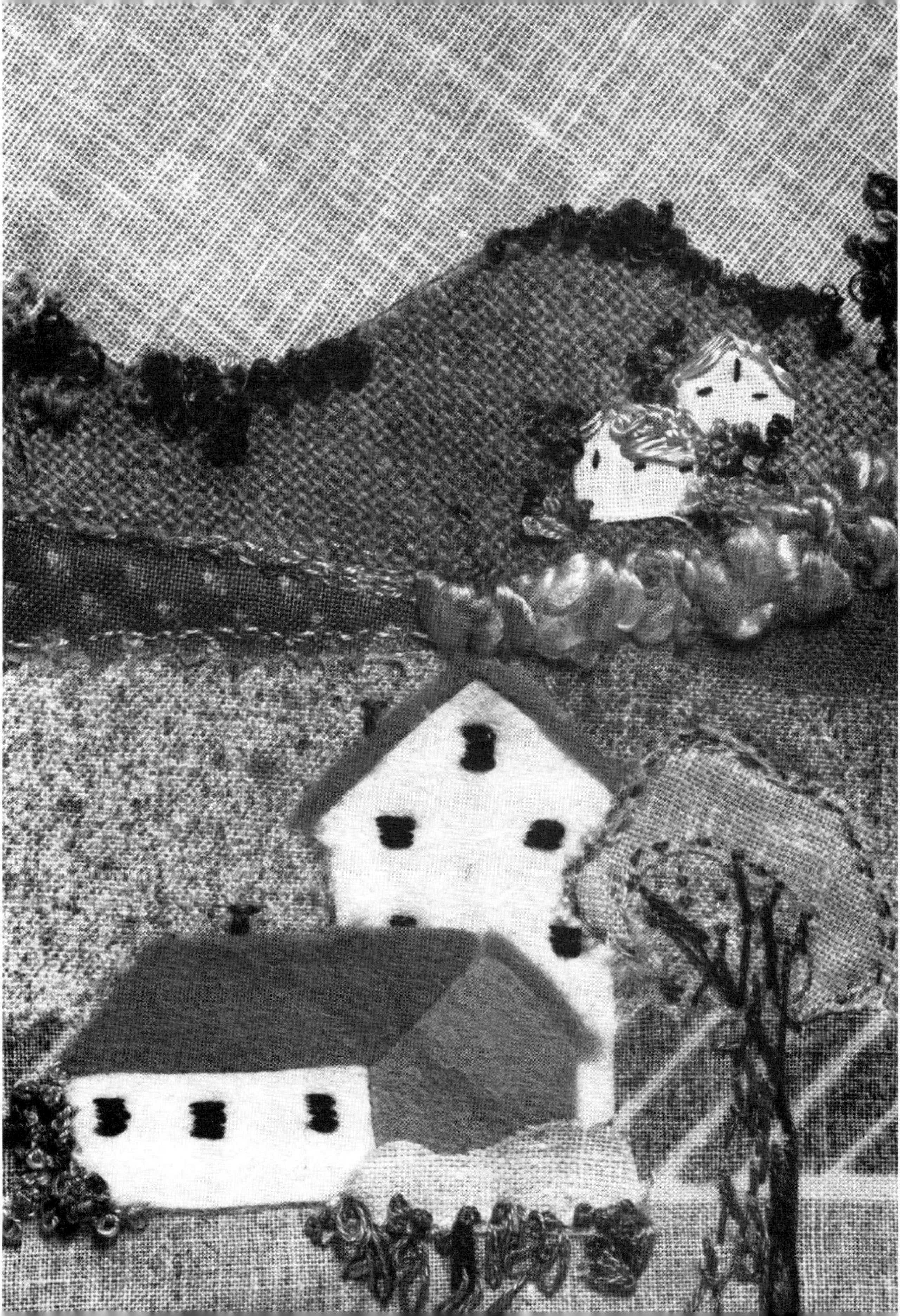

For larger, more complicated designs, make a collage. Collect an assortment of papers of all textures and varieties and use them to interpret the design. A viewfinder of card (see Chapter 2) will help to eliminate unwanted areas of the design. Remember to contrast the size of the shapes used–large and small ones make a much more interesting design than shapes that are all of the same size. Remember to have a focal point in your design. When you are happy with the result, interpret it in fabric. Try using fabrics that are all tones of the same colour, but vary the types and textures (this could work very well with a selection of fabrics all dyed together in the same dye bath). Vary the technique used, and add surface stitchery.

Fig. 51. In this tiny panel, felt has been used for the houses. In the background patterned as well as plain fabrics have been used, some applied diagonally to give added textural interest (Ann Johnson)

Six

Canvas work

Canvas work first became popular in Britain in the sixteenth century, although it was used for many years before. By this time. a large variety of different canvas stitches were in use, on samplers and hangings. During the Elizabethan and Stuart periods, table carpets and cushions became very popular, usually worked in tent stitch on extremely fine canvas.

Canvas work regained its popularity in Victorian times, with the invention of commercial dyes. Charts of designs were produced commercially for the first time. The embroideries were worked, usually in wools, and made into cushions, pictures, etc.

Today, canvas work has become a much more exciting form of embroidery, using a variety of canvasses and threads and combining embroidery with applied fabrics, fabric paint, etc. It is still fairly time-consuming, and, when completed, becomes a hard-wearing piece of fabric. It is, therefore, particularly suitable for practical objects, such as cushions, chair seats, rugs and church kneelers.

Materials

There are many different types of canvas available today. On the whole, single mesh canvas is much more versatile and easier to use than the double mesh type (called Penelope). Cotton canvas is cheaper than linen and suitable for most work. It is usually coloured white or yellow. The more expensive linen canvas is hard-wearing and better suited to chair seats and kneelers. A type of plastic canvas is also available; it can be cut to shape and is especially useful for children's work. The canvas mesh comes in a large range of sizes, from about 25 threads to the inch (10 threads per cm) to very large rug canvas.

Threads

Traditionally, wools were used for canvas work. However, it is much more exciting to vary the threads you use. Try embroidery threads–coton à broder, perlés, stranded cottons, silks, lurex and knitting wools. The only rules are that the threads should be smooth and fine enough to pass through the holes of the chosen canvas. On some projects, such as kneelers or chair seats, wools need to be used, and there are several types available to the embroiderer. 'Tapestry' is a single thread, usually quite thick and often difficult to use on finer mesh canvas. Crewel wools are sold in thinner strands and are altogether easier to use. Several strands can be threaded together through the needle to suit the mesh of the canvas, and strands of different colours can be used together to obtain a wider range of colour tones.

Needles should be 'tapestry'–blunt-ended to avoid snagging the canvas.

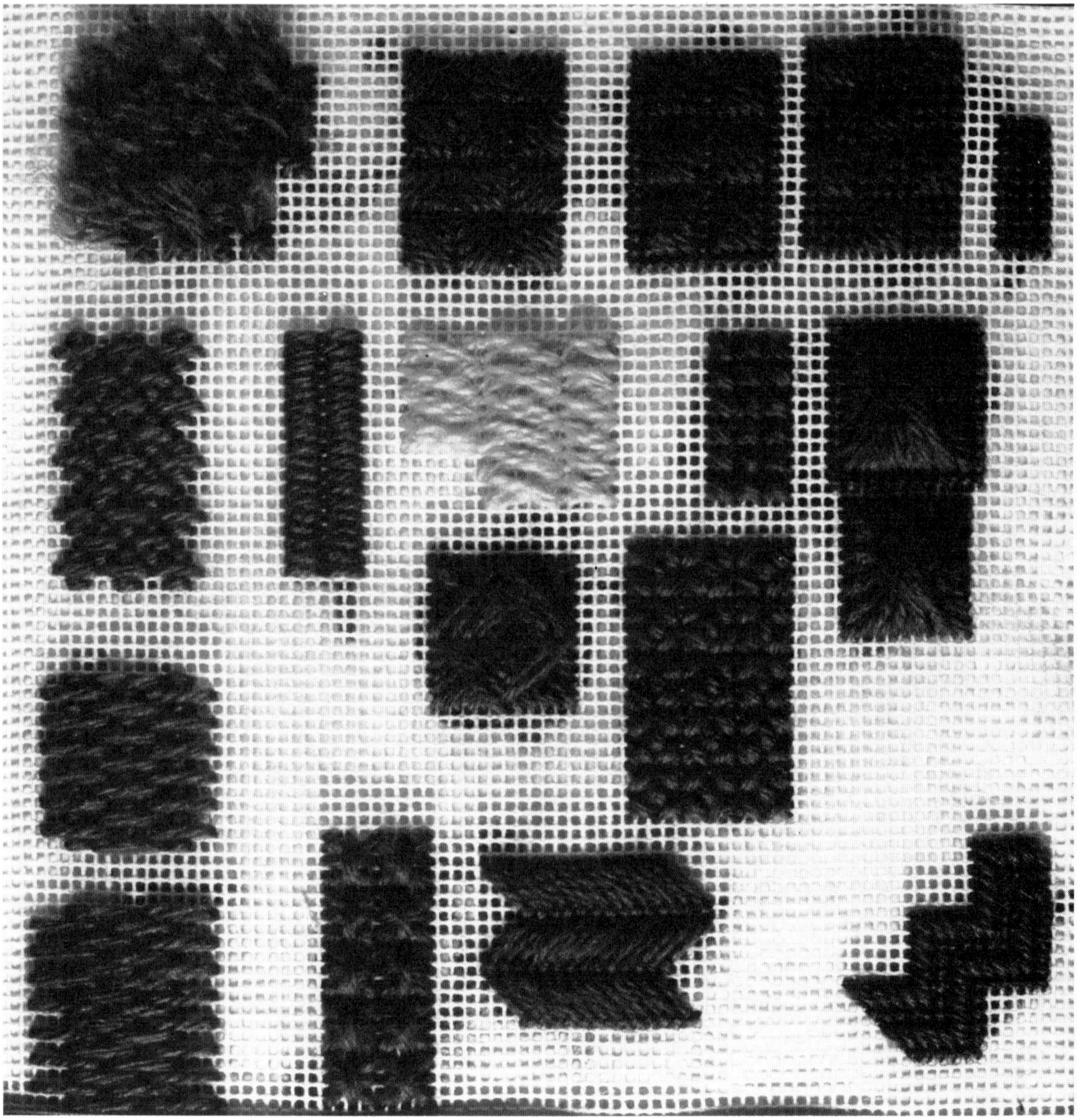

Fig. 52. Canvas stitches. Vertically, from top left: a) tent b) chequer c) Scottish d) mosaic e) velvet f) rhodes g) cross and rice stitch h) oblong cross i) satin j) Hungarian k) Jacquard l) fishbone m) Smyrna n) Parisian o) Gobelin

Frames

On the whole, canvas embroidery is best worked in a square frame, especially when using obvious diagonal stitches, such as tent, which will distort the fabric and require a great deal of stretching when finished to bring it back to its original shape.

Sampler

It is a good idea to work a sampler to begin with, to try out different stitches and effects achieved with various threads. When finished, the sampler can be made up into a cushion or panel. Buy a medium weight (16–18 threads to the inch, 6–7 threads per cm) cotton canvas to begin with.

Decide on the finished size of the canvas and cut out, leaving at least 2 inches (5 cm) spare canvas on each side. To prevent the canvas from fraying, it should be neatened on all four sides. This can be done with a zigzag stitch on the sewing machine, attaching a fabric binding, or simply by folding a length of masking tape over the edges. It can be mounted onto a slate frame (Chapter 1) or on a simple square frame. Use drawing pins and pin the canvas firmly to the frame. Start at the centre point of two opposite sides and work out from this point; the pins should not be more than 2 inches (5 cm) apart.

Collect a variety of threads to use, remembering that they should all be smooth and pass easily through the canvas mesh. Just because this is a sampler and a first attempt, do not be tempted to think that any old scrap will do. Choose a colour scheme, or stick to tones of one colour. Contrast dull threads with shiny ones, and, if possible, add a small amount of lurex thread as well.

To begin, tie a knot in the end of the thread, and take the needle down through the canvas from the right side, a few threads away from where you wish to start. As you work towards the knot, you will cover the end on the wrong side so that the knot can be snipped off. To fasten off, run the needle through the previous stitches on the wrong side. Do not cut off too long a length of thread, especially when using wool, as it will wear and fray with the friction of the canvas.

Stitches

There are an enormous number of canvas stitches, which can be slightly offputting to the beginner. As with surface stitchery, restrict yourself to eight to ten stitches. Try to vary them in size; some stitches, e.g. tent, are worked over one or two threads of canvas. These are quite hard-wearing and would be suitable for practical objects. Others, worked over several threads, although exciting to work, are not so practical, as the long threads on the surface can snag and break. Some suitable stitches for the beginner to try are tent, cross, rice, cushion, Rhodes, Hungarian, jacquard, and velvet (which gives a lovely raised pile). There are, of course, many other stitches to be found in a dictionary, all of which can be used to good effect.

An interesting way of working a sampler, and one which makes a very satisfying design if the colour scheme is good, is to work different stitches in rows straight across the canvas. Start with a fairly simple stitch, such as rice, and work one or two rows in one colour. Below that, work another row of rice stitch, but this time cross the corners in a contrasting thread. Continue working in this way down the length of the canvas, using different stitches. Vary the length of each band to make the finished work look more interesting. The same stitch could be worked several times, but using different threads and colours each time.

Alternatively, start the sampler in the centre and work outwards. Choose a distinctive stitch, such as Rhodes, to put in the middle. Surround it with a row (on all four sides) of a small, compact stitch, simple cross perhaps, and continue to work outwards, changing stitches and threads, but keeping all four sides identical.

When completed, you will find that, provided you have kept to a restricted colour scheme, the sampler will look good enough to be framed into a panel or cushion. If it has been worked without using a frame, it will almost certainly need to be stretched back into shape (see Chapter 8).

Using stitches to make a design is an extremely effective method of creating canvas work. If different stitches are used together, they almost automatically provide texture–for example, tent, rice, velvet, gobelin.

Provided that it is not intended to be used for practical purposes, beads, sequins, leathers, etc., can all be applied to canvas. Ribbons and textured threads can be couched on to the surface. It is not always necessary to cover the entire surface with stitchery: fabric paints can be applied with great effect.

Experiment with stitches: try greatly enlarging the size of the stitch, or working the stitches in unusual threads. Surface stitchery can also be used on canvas–use linear stitches and isolated stitches such as french knots. Buildings and all geometric forms provide wonderful inspiration for canvas work, but ideas from gardens, flowers and landscapes can also be used to great effect.

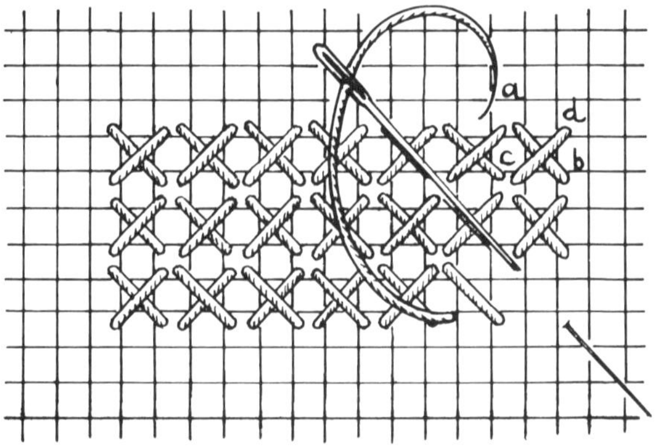

Fig. 53. Cross stitch. Bring needle up though the canvas at A and insert at B. Bring the needle up again at C and re-insert at D. Each stitch should be completed before moving on to the next stitch

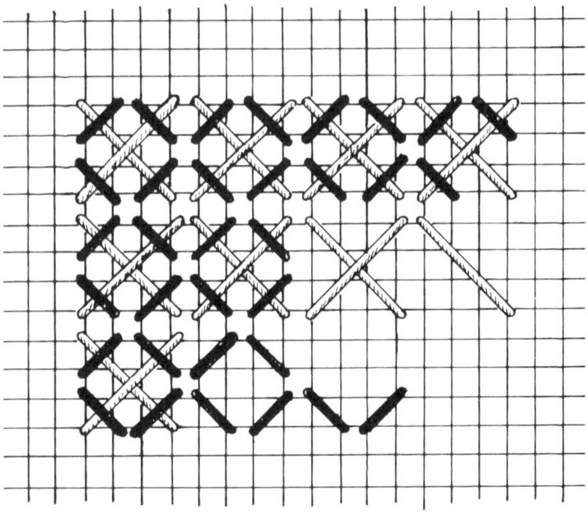

Fig. 54. Rice stitch, or crossed corners. First work a cross stitch as in Fig. 53. Then work four small diagonal stitches over each corner. This stitch is effective if the crossed corners are worked in a contrast thread

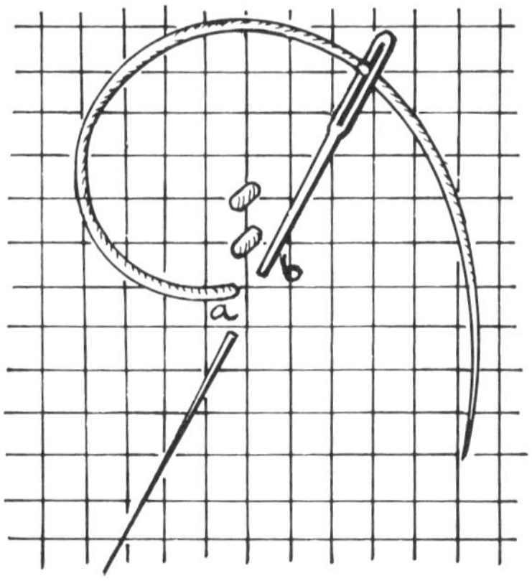

Fig. 55. Tent stitch. A tiny stitch worked over just one intersection of the canvas. Bring the needle up through the canvas at A and re-insert at B

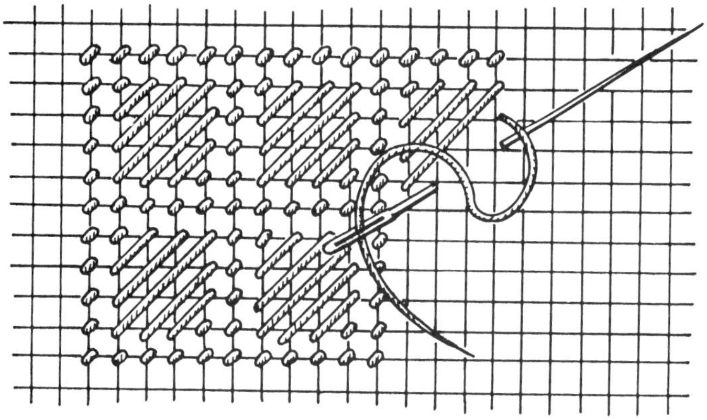

Fig. 56. Scottish stitch. A set of diagonal stitches are worked over one, two, three, then two and one intersections of the canvas. The squares are surrounded by a row of tent stitches, which could be worked in a contrasting or toning thread

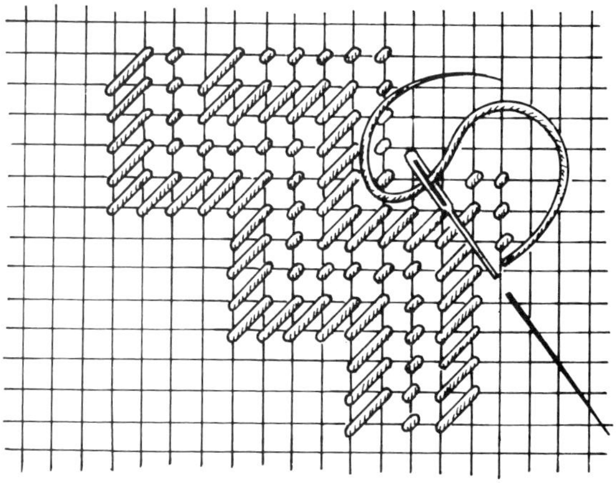

Fig. 57. Jacquard. The first row consists of a 'step' pattern of a diagonal stitch worked over two threads of the canvas. On either side of this are worked rows of tent stitch, following the 'stepped' arrangement

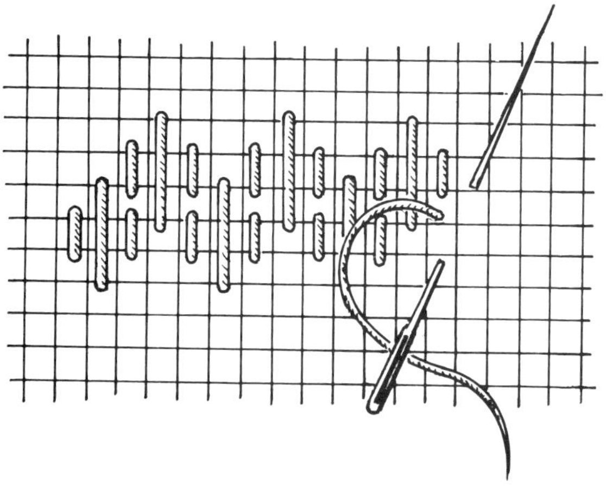

Fig. 58. Hungarian stitch. Small vertical stitches are worked over two, then three, then two threads of the canvas. Leave two threads unworked between each group of stitches. The second row of stitches will interlock neatly

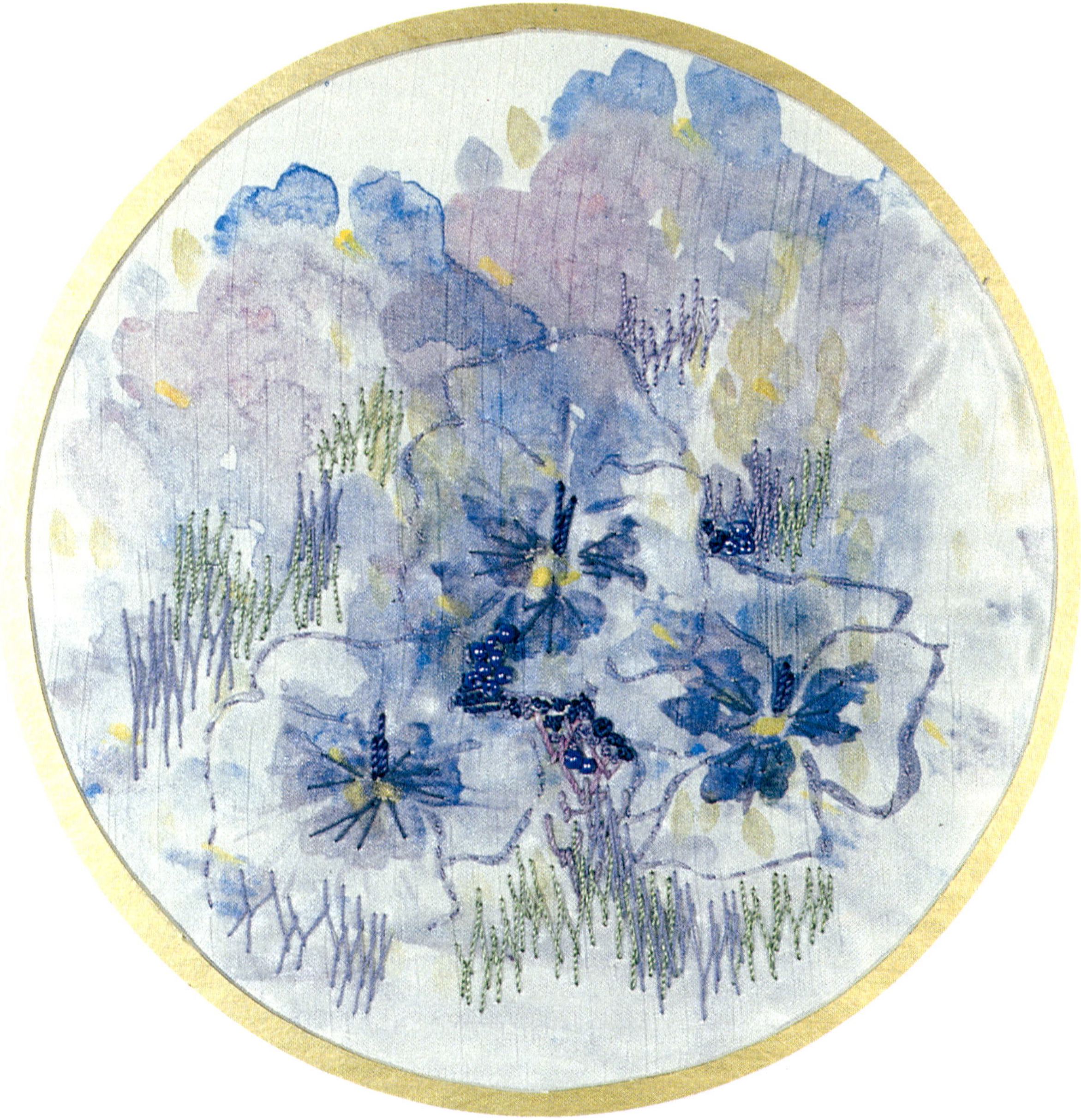

1. Design based on drawings of pansies. The flowers have been printed on to the background fabric with transfer paints. Some of the flowers have been outlined in running stitch and beads; french knots and cretan stitch have been used to enhance the delicacy of the design (Frances Roche)

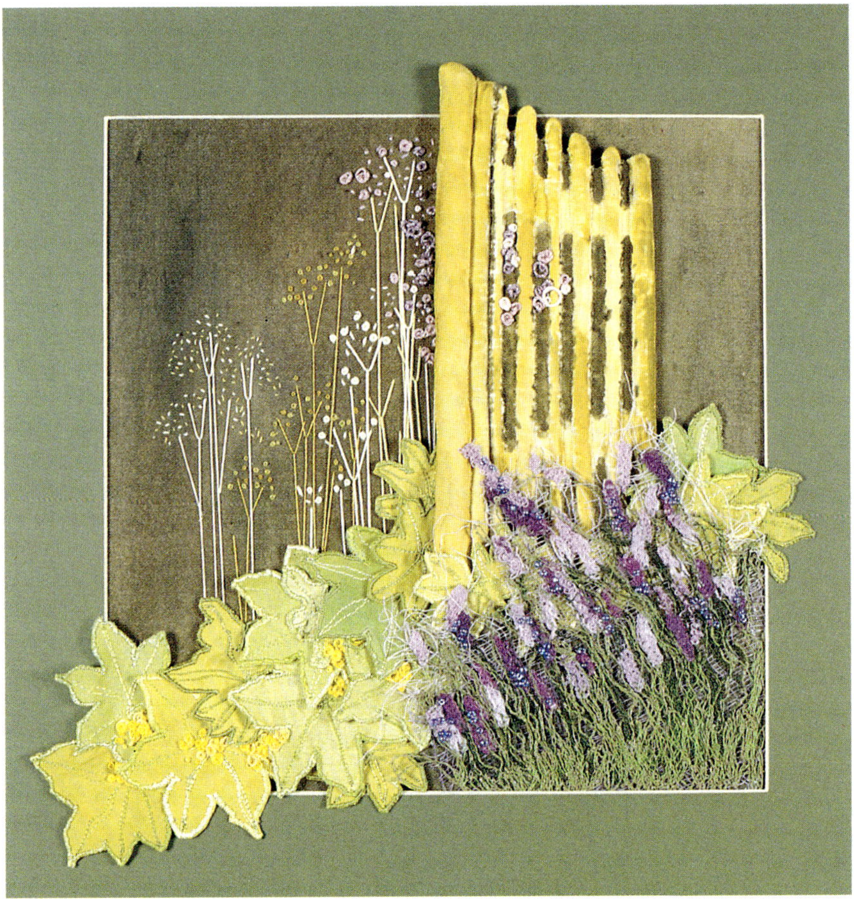

2. Small panel inspired by a magazine illustration. The gate has been painted, quilted and applied to the dyed background fabric. The leaves have also been cut out and applied separately to the design. Surface stitches and some machine embroidery have been added (Barbara Mellor)

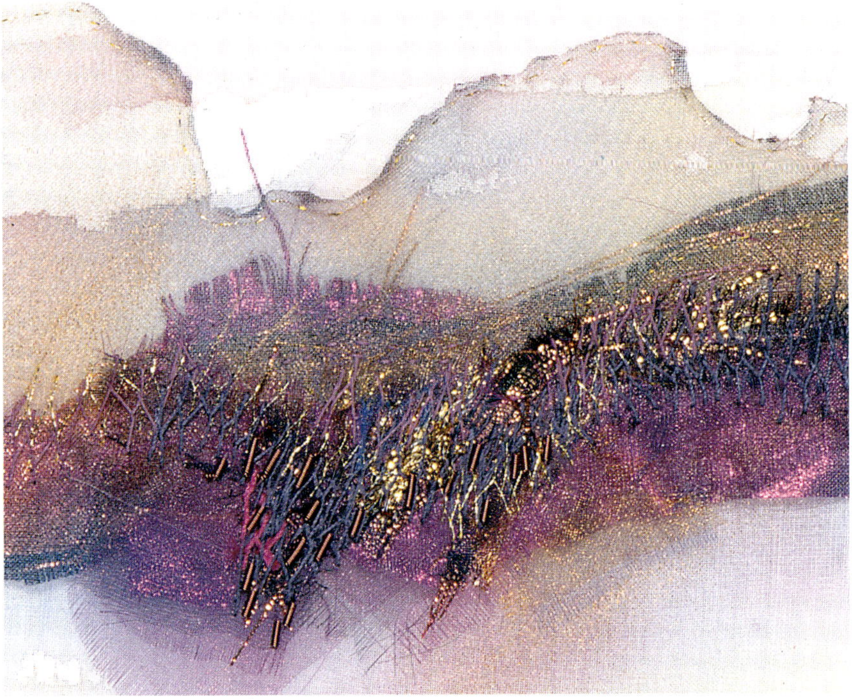

3. Shadow work based on drawings of heather-covered moors. The silk organza has been dyed and fabrics, including lurex, have been applied to the underneath as well as to the right side of the work. The edges of the applied fabrics have been frayed or burnt. The stitchery is mostly cretan stitch in silks and lurex thread (Jenny Bullen)

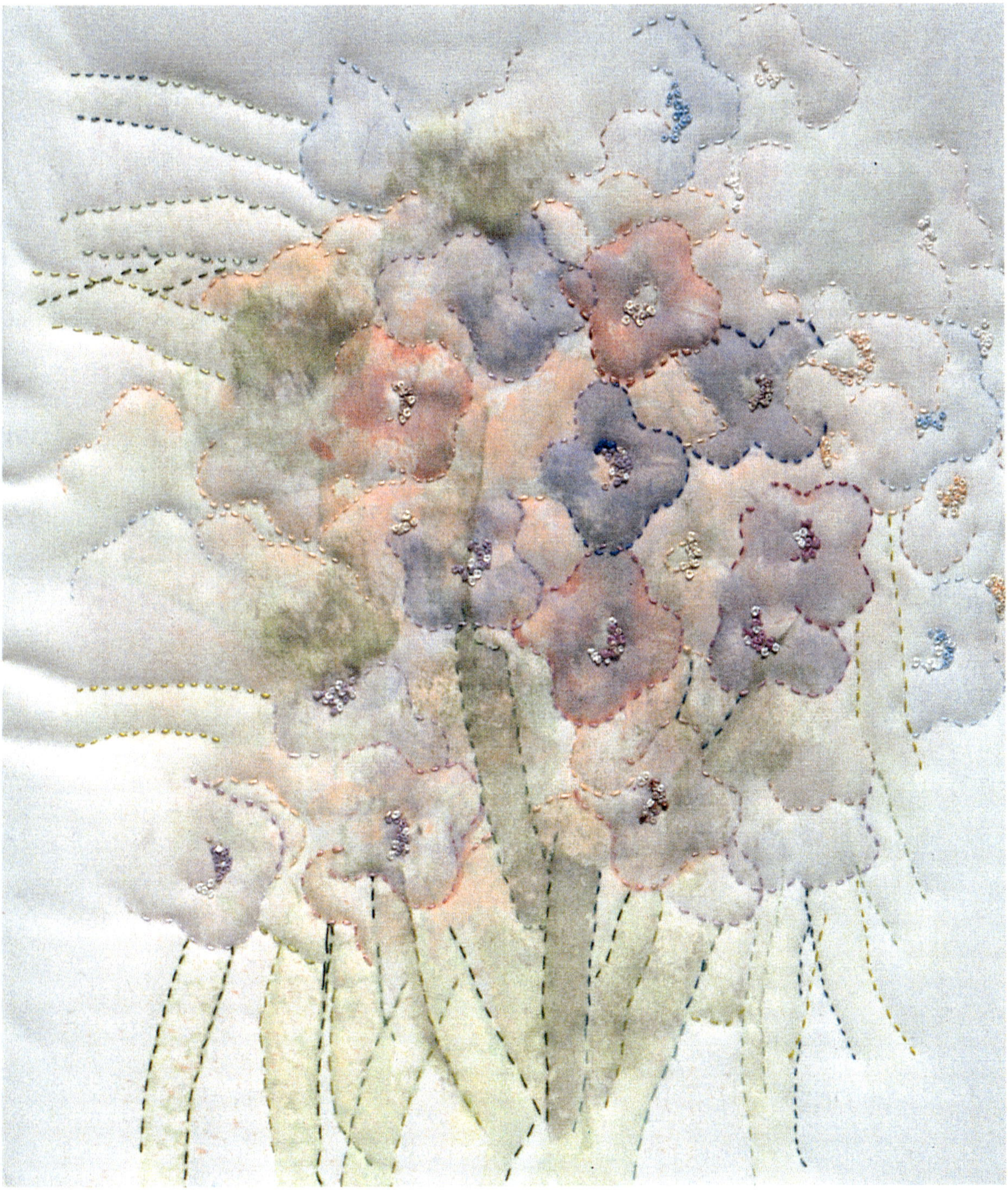

4. The tops of egg boxes have been used to print a design with transfer paints reminiscent of a bunch of flowers. The design has been quilted using coloured threads, and french knots added to some of the 'flower' centres (Ann Johnson)

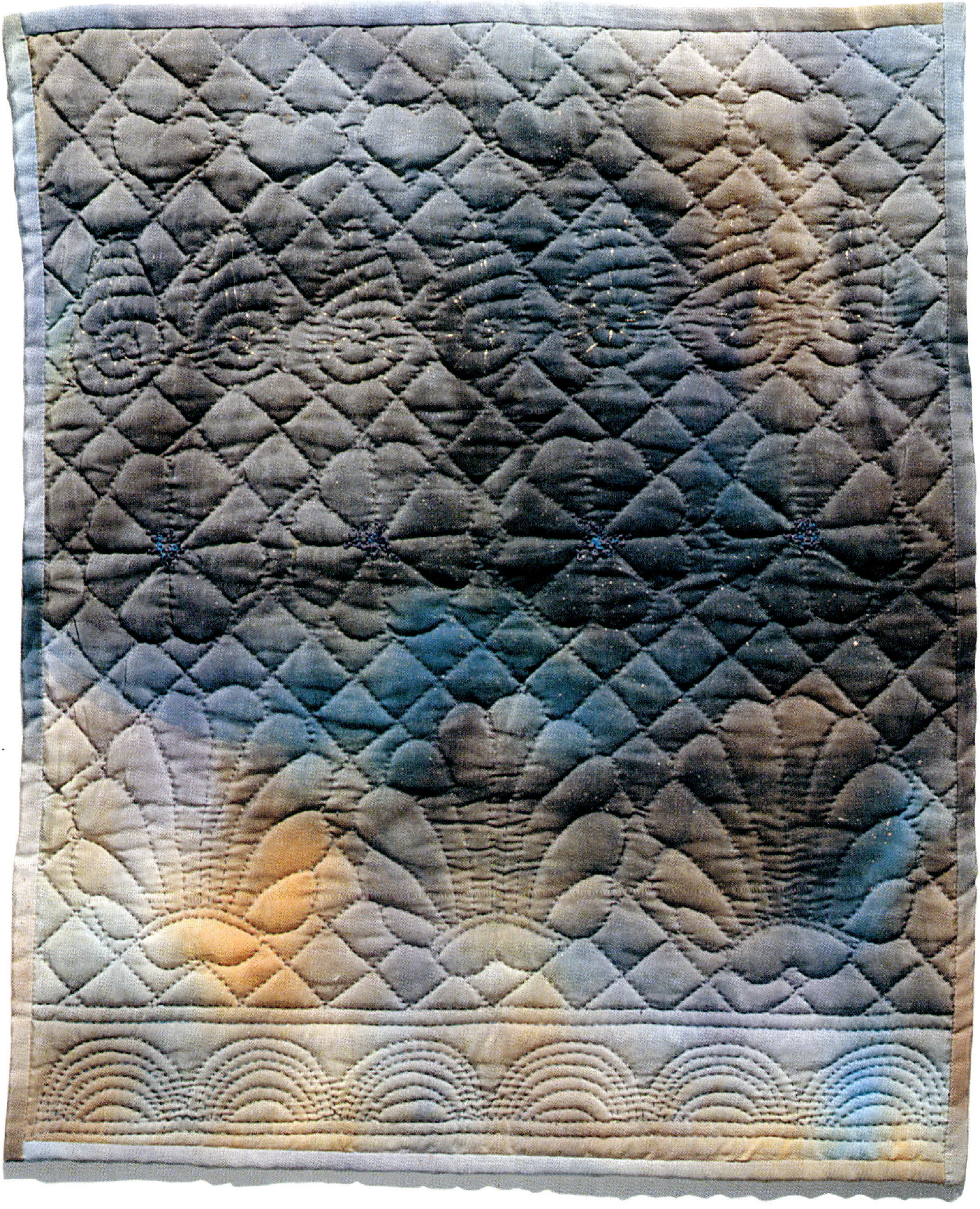

5. A small quilted hanging using traditional quilt motifs to form a design. Fabric paints were first sponged on to a piece of silk fabric. The quilting has been carried out in running stitch using silk threads. A small amount of gold lurex thread has been added in places to highlight the design (Jenny Bullen)

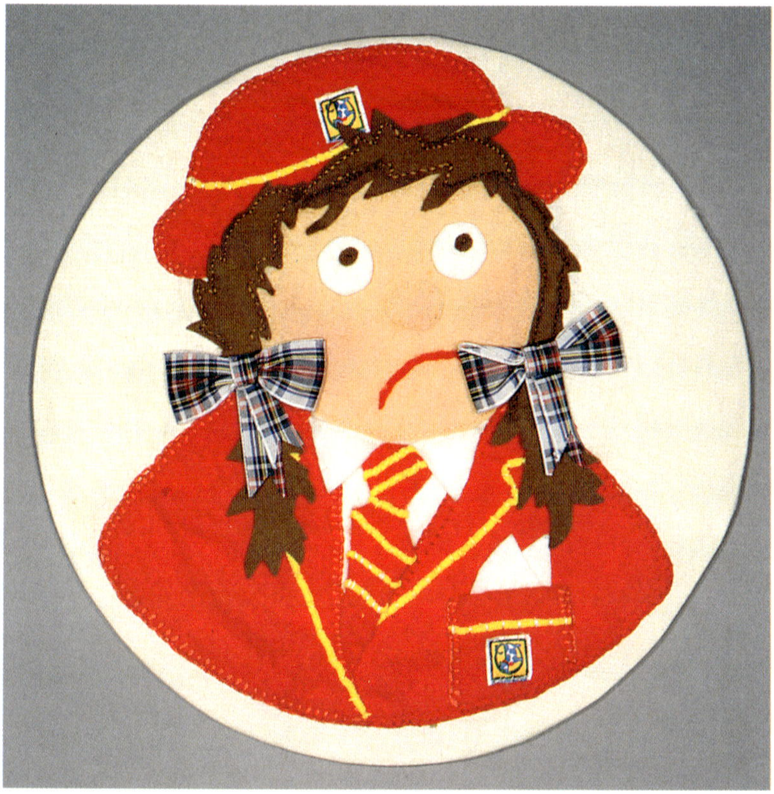

6. *Beryl,* a portrait. Coloured felts have been cut out and applied to a felt background, using a variety of hand stitches. The tartan hair ribbons are three-dimensional (Emma Johnson, aged 12)

7. A colourful canvas work pincushion worked in a variety of threads, including silks, lurex and wool. The top is worked in Scottish stitch and the sides in cross stitch (Jennifer Murray)

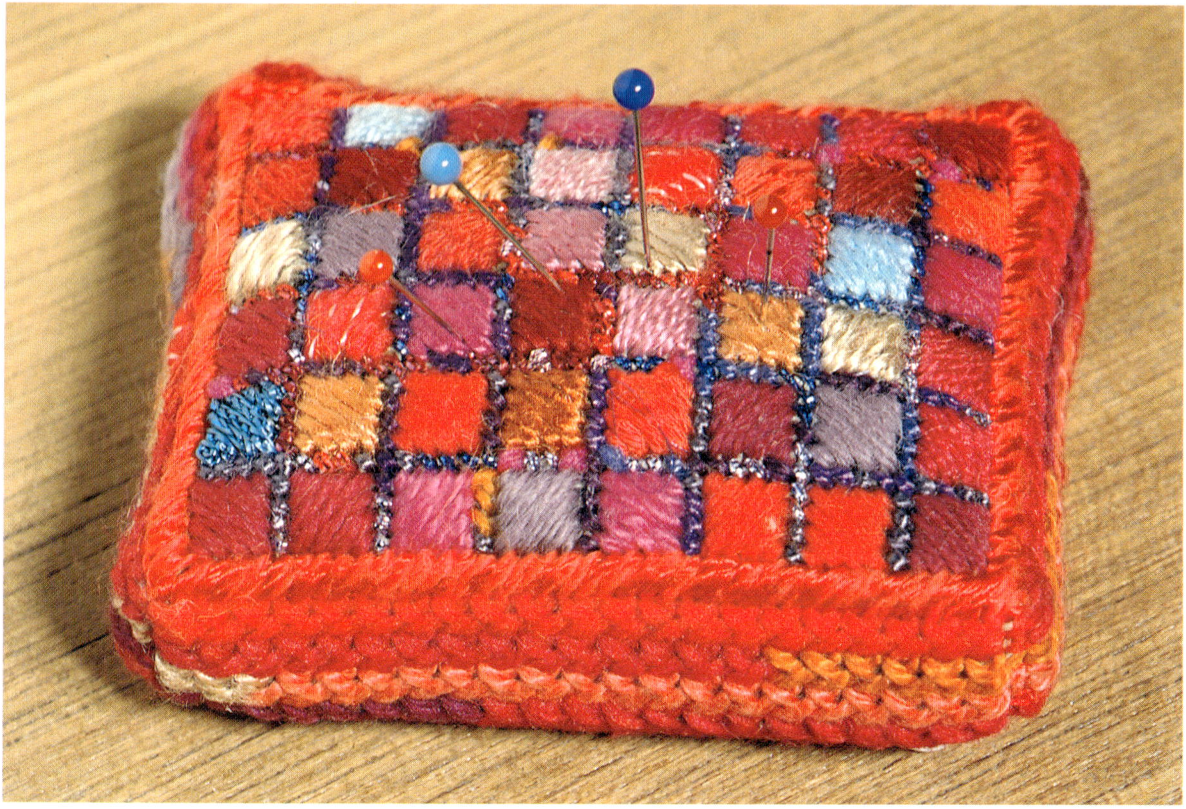

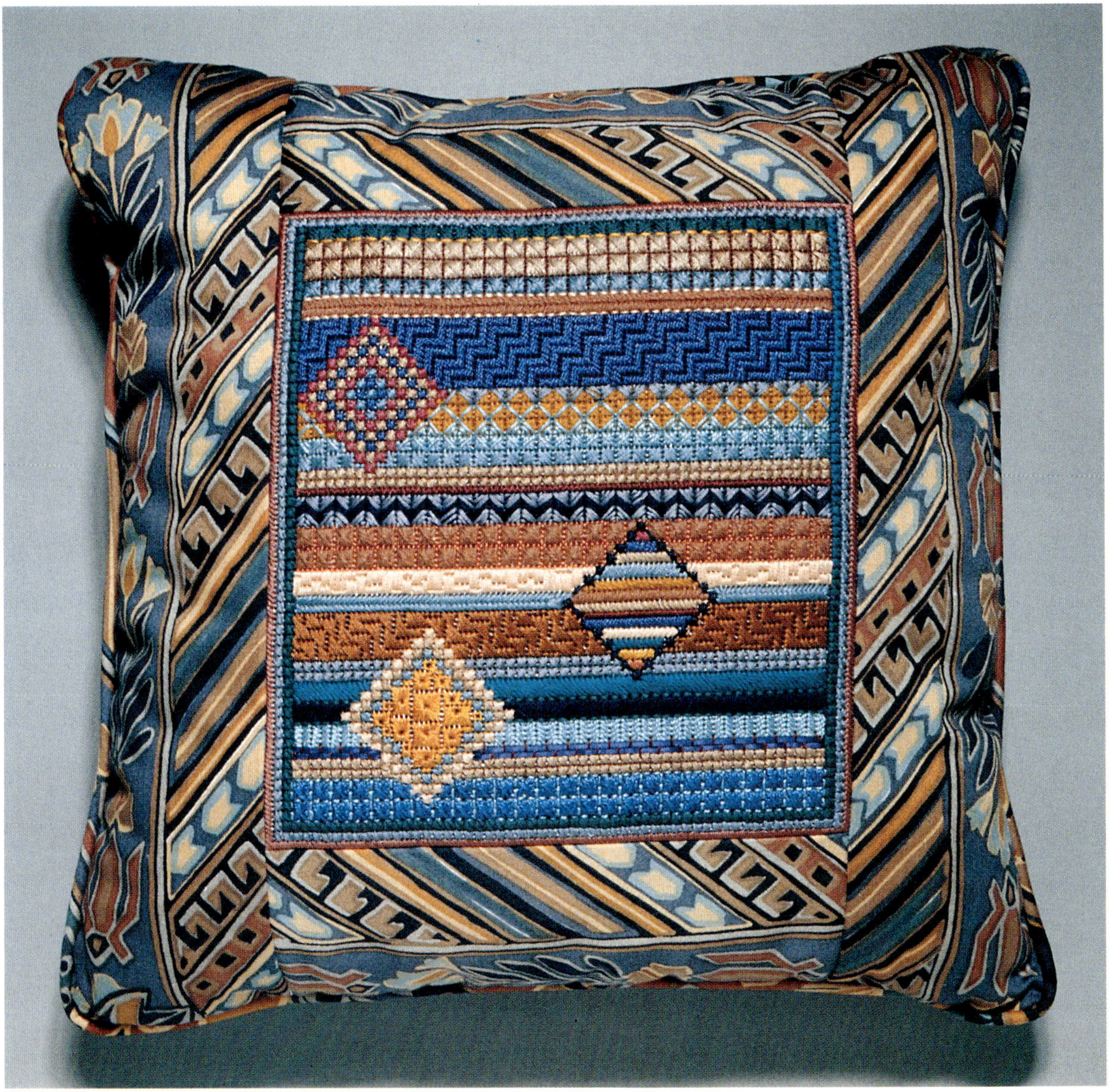

8. A cushion in canvas work with patterned fabric surround. The embroidery threads, mostly stranded cottons and perlés, have been exactly matched to the colours in the fabric. Stitches include cross stitch, jacquard, Rhodes and tent (Ann Le-Moignan)

9. A canvas work garden. The canvas has first been painted and quite large areas have been left unworked. Coloured organza has been applied to part of the design. Stitches used include tent, cross, straight stitch, and french knots (Frances Roche)

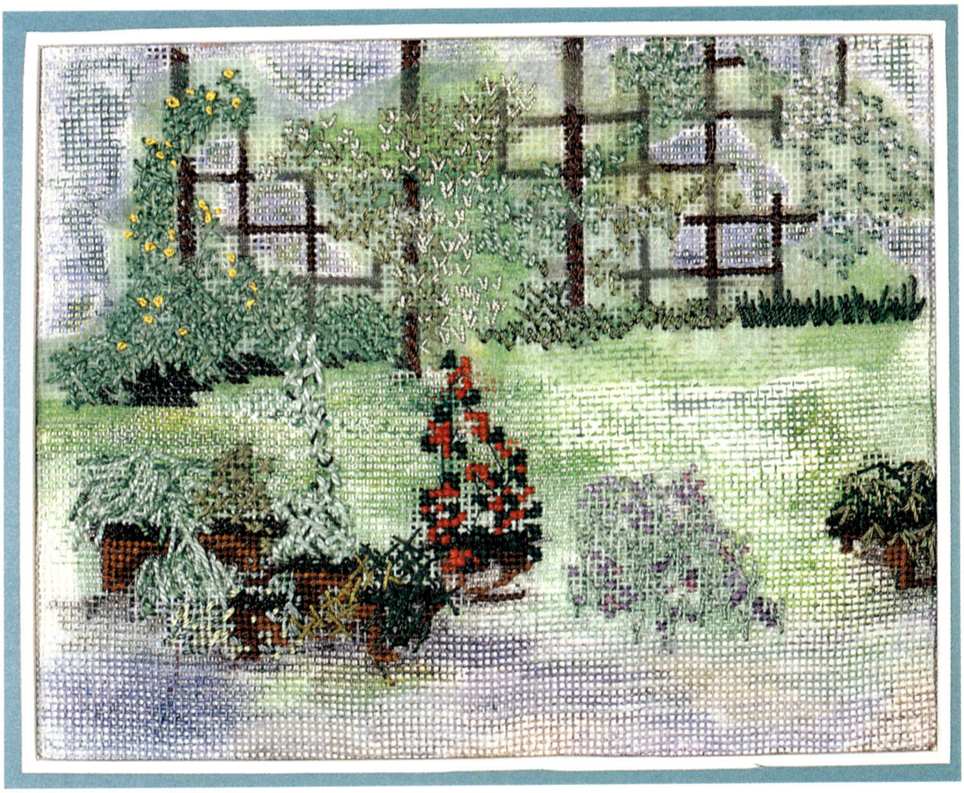

10. A colourful panel worked entirely in cross stitch and based on the designs found on a Bedouin (Arab) dress. Stranded cottons have been used to work the embroidery (Diana Mitchell)

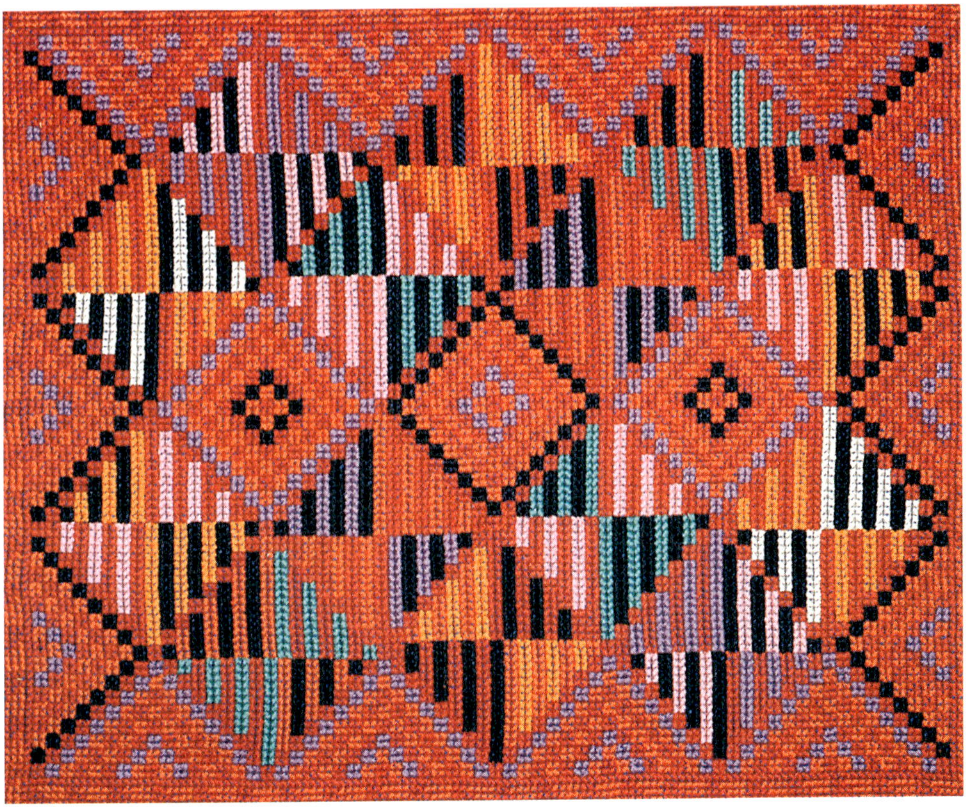

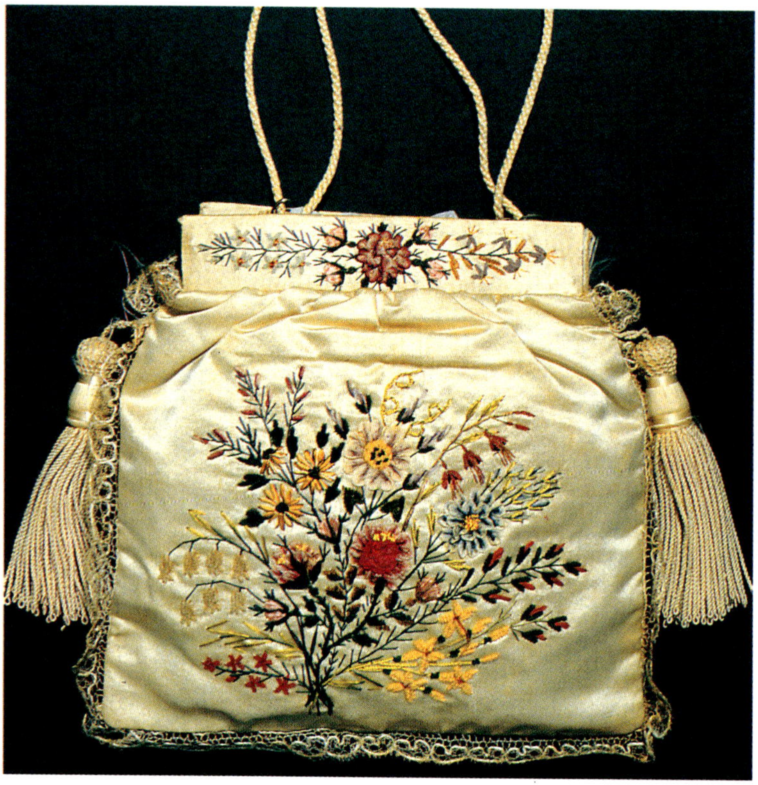

11. An exquisite early nineteenth-century ribbon work-bag. The embroidery has been worked on cream satin and has been trimmed with a delicate lace edging. The silk tassels have been worked over wooden moulds

12. A cushion in counted thread work, based on an imaginary landscape, surrounded by small cameos of flowers. The stitches include darning, cross stitch and double running. The embroidery has been carried out in perlé threads (Eleanor Dunphy)

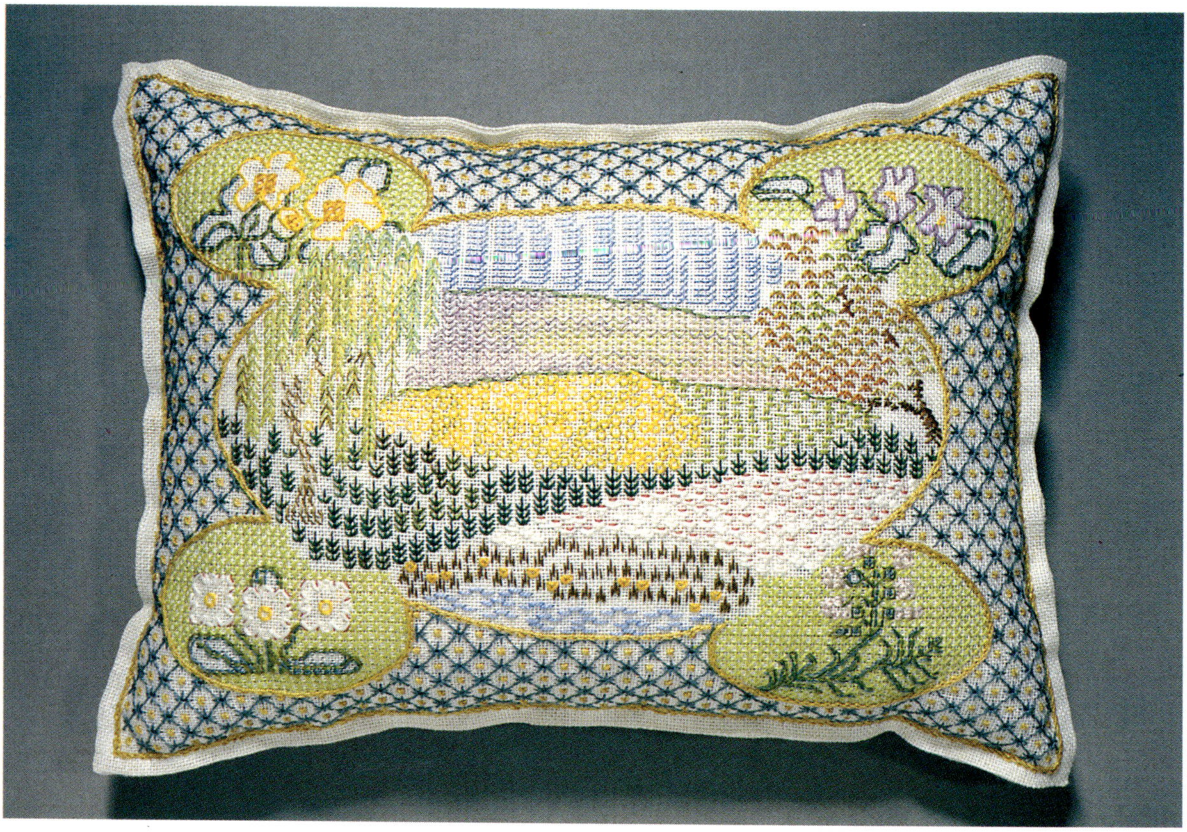

Fig. 59. Rhodes stitch. A large stitch which can be worked over any number of threads of the canvas. Bring the needle up at A and insert at B. Bring the needle out again at C and re-insert at D. Bring the needle out again at E and continue to work in this way until the square has been completed. The stitch is particularly effective if worked in a randomly dyed thread

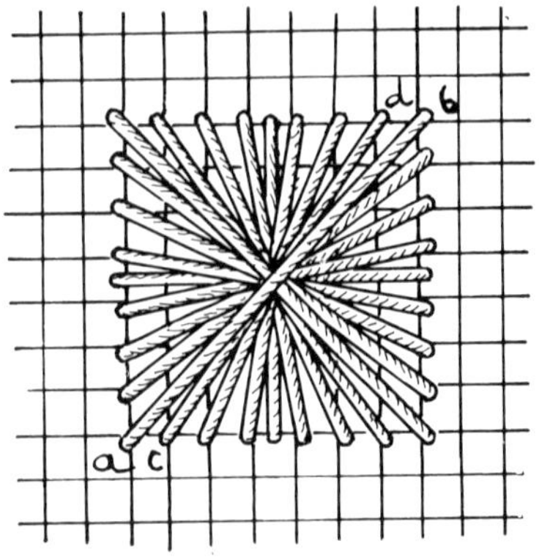

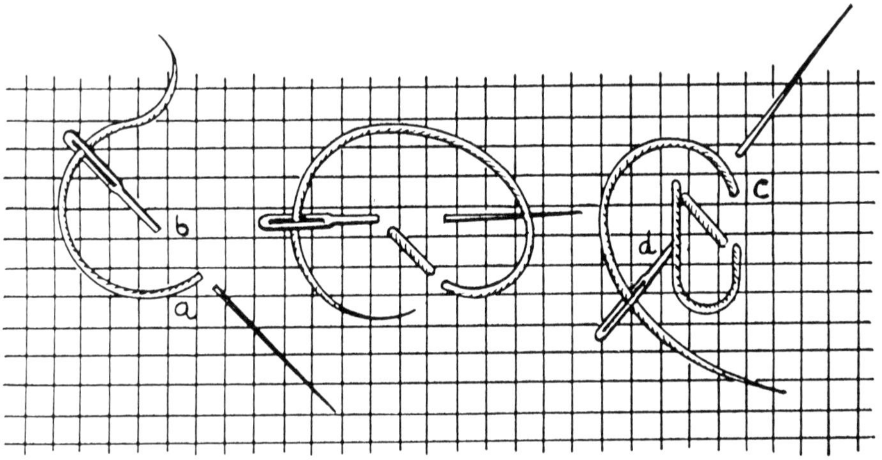

Fig. 60. Velvet stitch. Bring the needle up through the canvas at A and insert at B. Bring the needle out again at A and re-insert at B, but this time leaving a loop of thread on the surface. Bring the needle out at C and re-insert at D. When all the stitches have been worked the loops are cut and trimmed. This stitch is best worked in wool

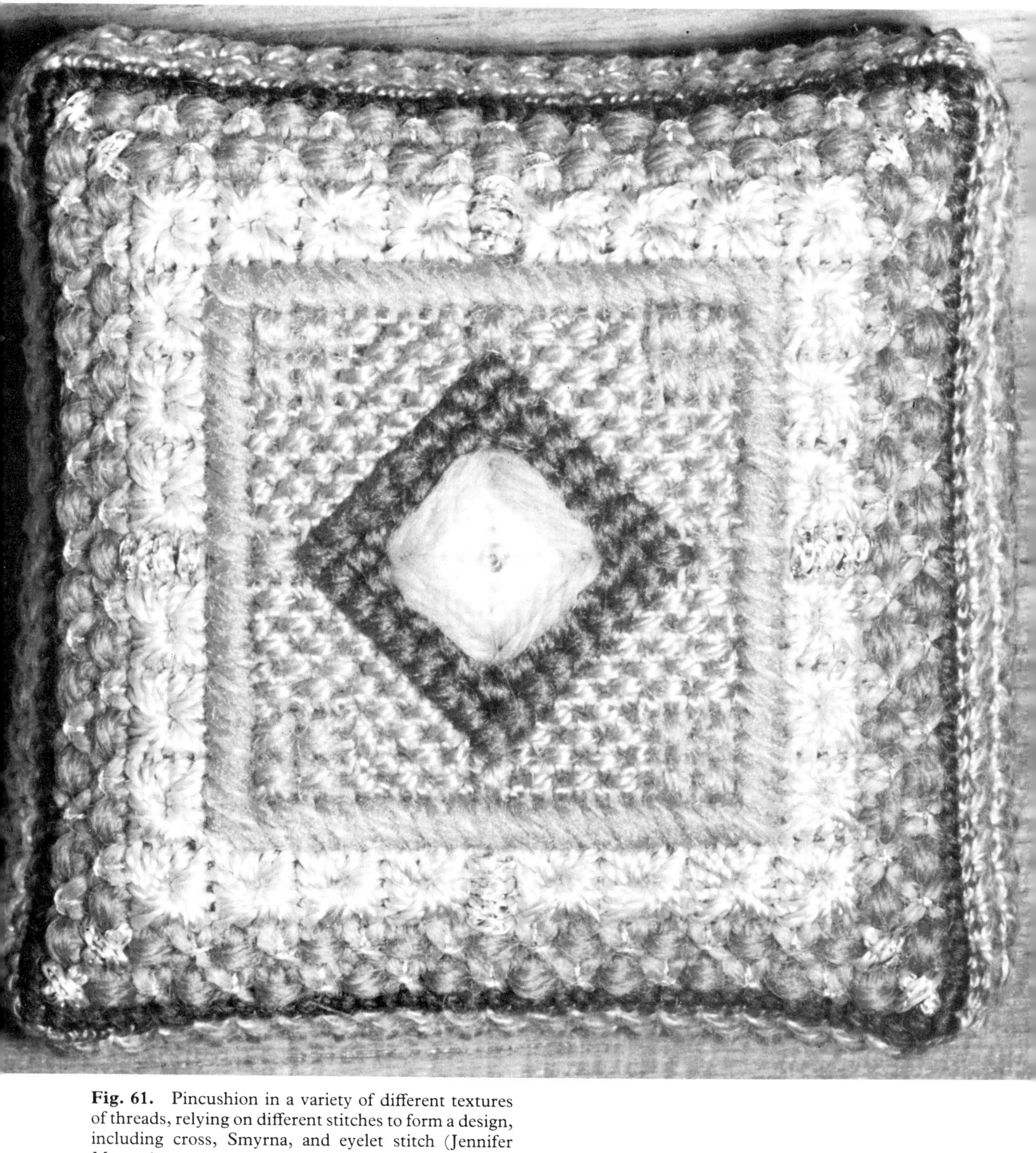

Fig. 61. Pincushion in a variety of different textures of threads, relying on different stitches to form a design, including cross, Smyrna, and eyelet stitch (Jennifer Murray)

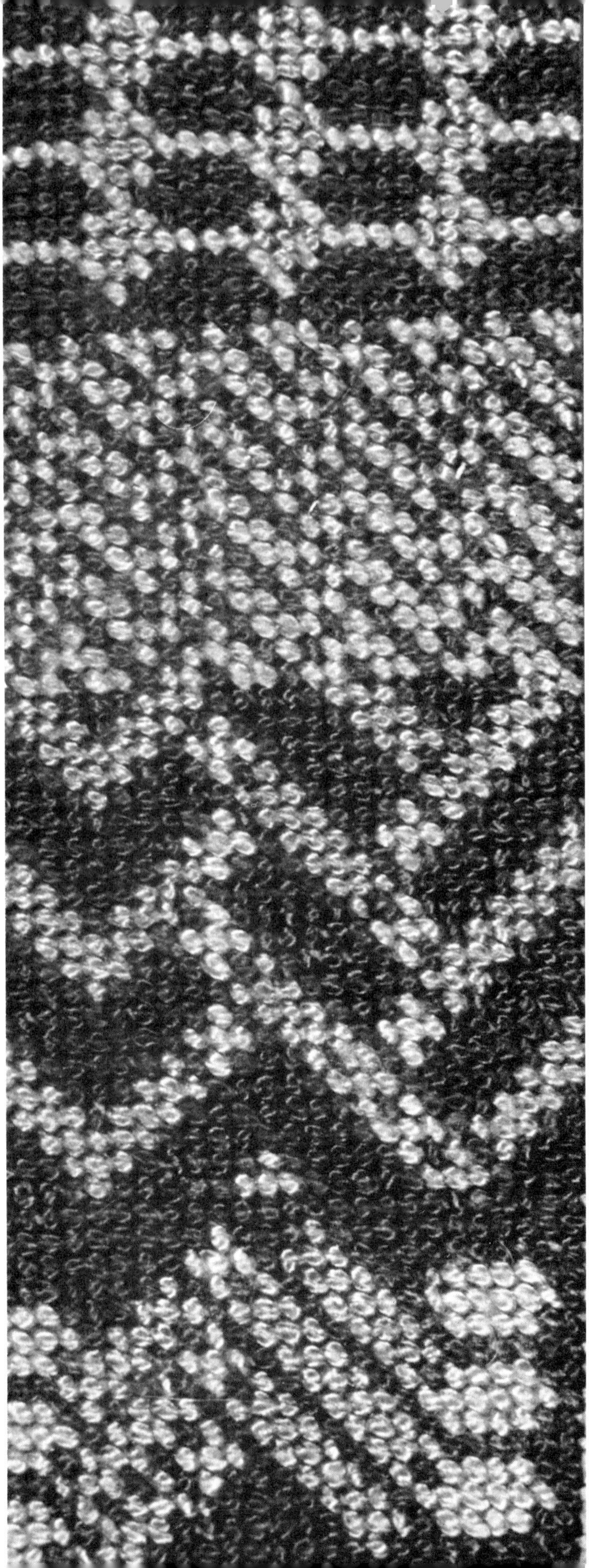

Fig. 62. Small sampler of tent stitch, based on the patterns on Tudor chimneys at Hampton Court, worked in stranded cottons in shades of terracotta and cream (Diana Mitchell)

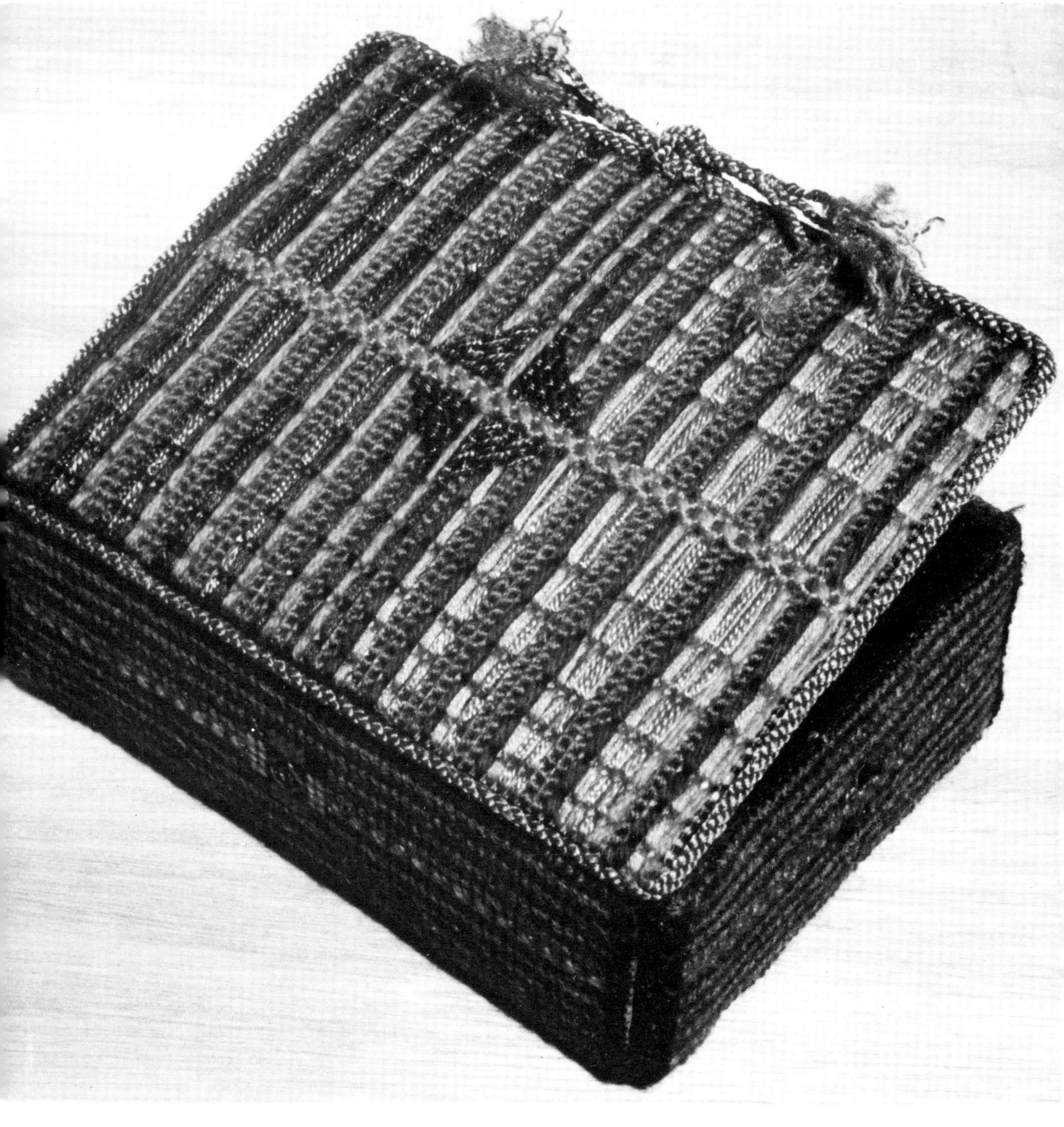

Fig. 63. Box made of plastic canvas and edged with a shiny twisted cord. Stitches include straight and cross stitch (Margaret Beazley)

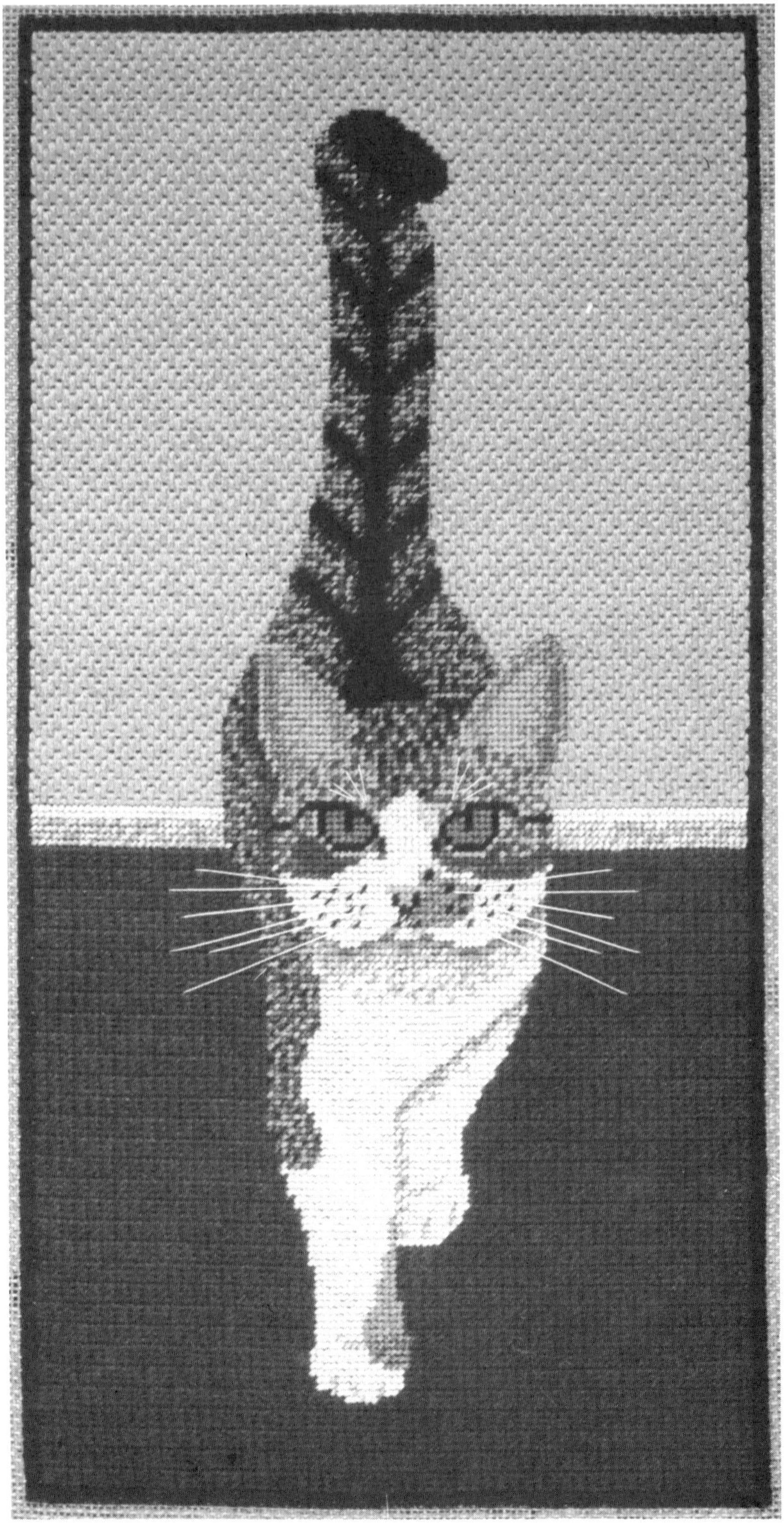

Fig. 64. A portrait of the embroiderer's tabby cat. The cat has been worked entirely in tent stitch with other stitches producing a contrast of texture for the background (Alison Dummer)

Seven

Counted thread embroidery

Counted thread work encompasses a large number of embroidery techniques, and it would not be possible to cover all of them in a general embroidery book. In this chapter some of the simpler techniques, which can, however, be used to great effect, are described. Other counted thread techniques which can be investigated are pulled work, drawn thread work and Hardanger.

Materials

Counted thread embroidery is often used on practical articles, such as table linen. It is, therefore, worth investing in a good quality fabric–linen or cotton–with a base of threads that can be easily counted by the eye. Threads used should be smooth and pass easily through the fabric, such as coton à broder, perlés, Flower threads and linen embroidery threads. Tapestry needles should be used.

It is not necessary to use a frame, but the edges of the fabric should be secured to prevent unravelling, either with a zigzag stitch on the sewing machine, or overcast by hand.

Transferring the design to the fabric

Tracing and tacking is probably the most suitable method.

Pattern darning

Pattern darning is an extremely simple but very effective technique. It consists of a simple running stitch, picking up a regular number of threads on an evenweave background. By varying which threads are picked up, quite complicated patterns can be achieved.

Work a small sampler of different patterns on an evenweave ground. Use two or three contrasting threads.

Darning can be used with great effect in conjunction with fabric paints or printing. Try printing with objects such as pieces of polystyrene, egg boxes or torn card, to build up a background for stitchery. Match the threads to the colours of the fabric paints, perhaps varying the thicknesses. Build up areas of pattern within the shapes, but do not overwhelm the design with stitchery; the stitches should enhance rather than dominate the embroidery. Remember that the stitches can be worked in horizontal, vertical and diagonal lines. Tiny beads, scraps of organza, or a tiny glint of metal thread could be added.

This type of design would be more suitable for a small panel than for practical purposes, but it could be made into an exquisite little bag.

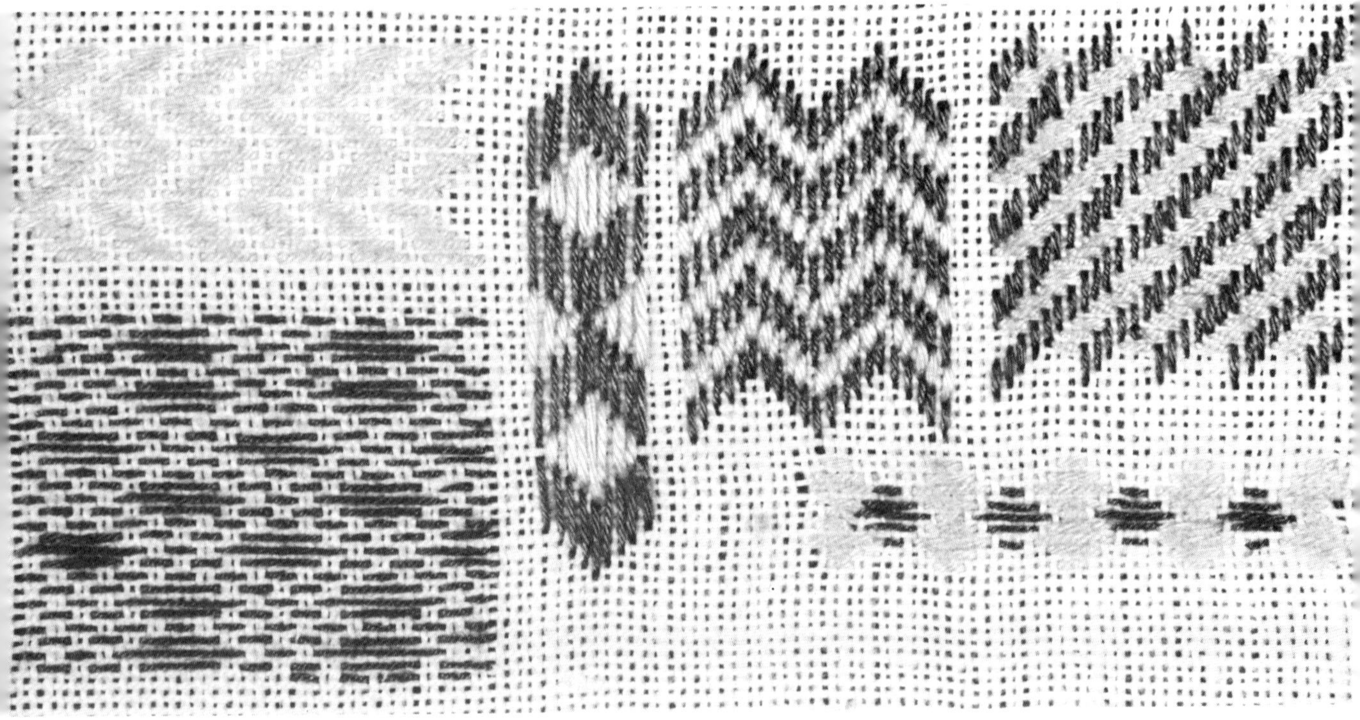

Fig. 65. Pattern darning sampler (Nancy Woodman)

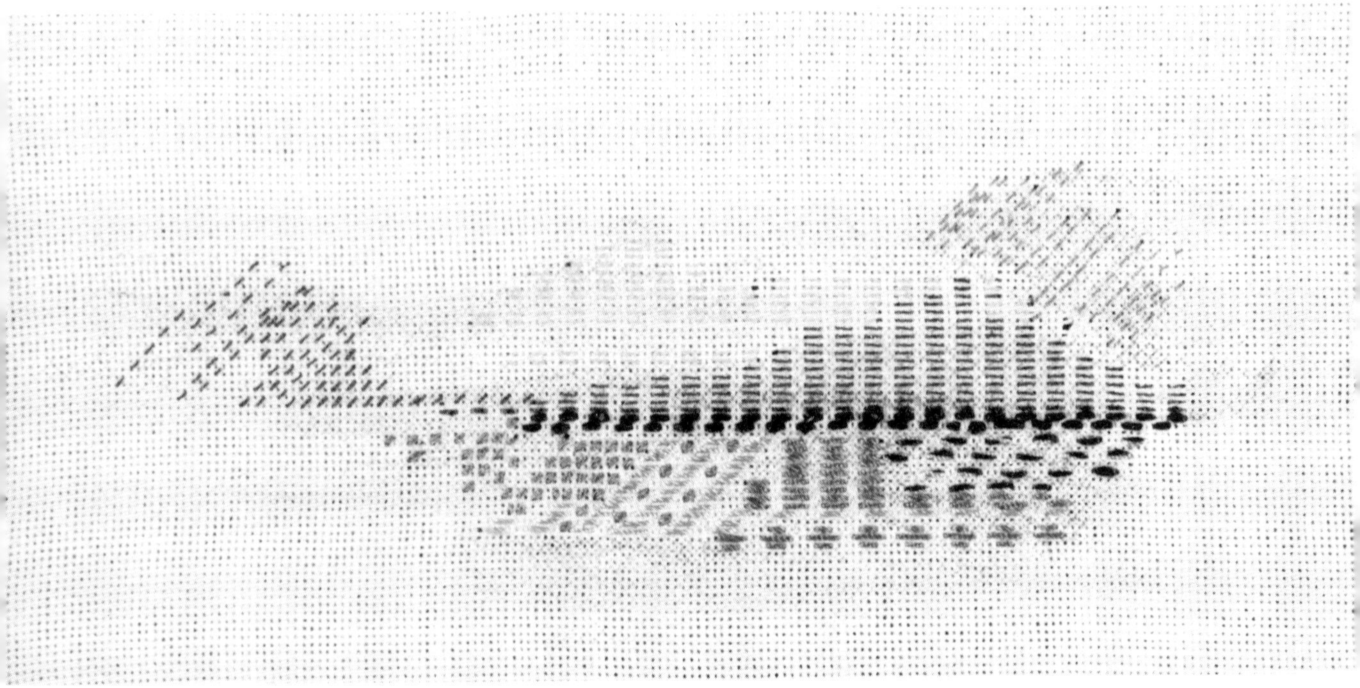

Fig. 66. Pattern darning used to produce a tiny landscape. The evenweave linen was lightly painted before stitching. Some of the stitches have been worked diagonally (Barbara Mellor)

Cross stitch

Cross stitch is another extremely effective technique which is very simple to work. It should be stitched on an evenweave fabric, but this can vary from coarse hessian, canvas and 'Binca' type fabrics, to very fine linens. Threads should match the fabric in thickness and be smooth. Interesting effects can be obtained by using matt and shiny threads in the same piece of work. Simple borders can be used on table linens and cushions using just one or two carefully chosen colours.

Try taking your own design from a photograph or drawing, and converting it to a pattern on graph paper. Lay a sheet of tracing paper over the photograph and trace off the outlines. Try not to make the design too complicated. Transfer the outline to graph paper and square it up. One square of graph paper will be the equivalent to one cross stitch.

Embroider a flower garden in cross stitch. Choose a photograph that has some bright areas, but some dull, quiet areas as well. Pick out the colours in threads, then build up an all-over pattern in cross stitch using the appropriate colours. Use shiny threads and matt threads so that some parts of the design will stand out. To merge areas of colour, different coloured threads can be used together in the needle. With such a large concentration of stitchery, it will probably be easier to work this in a frame.

Cross stitch can be worked on a closely woven fabric if desired. Tack a piece of evenweave fabric across the chosen fabric, being careful to match the grain lines where possible. Use a sharp pointed needle, and work the cross stitch through both fabrics. When the embroidery has been completed, the evenweave fabric should be carefully pulled away, thread by thread. In some specialist shops it is possible to buy an evenweave fabric especially for this purpose.

Holbein stitch

Holbein stitch, or double running, is often used in conjunction with other counted thread techniques, but is effective when used by itself to build up quite complicated designs. It is a regular, counted thread running stitch worked in two stages. First of all, a running stitch is worked over an even number of threads, the spaces left between the stitches being the same size as the stitches themselves. On the return journey the spaces are filled in to produce a dense linear stitch. It is traditionally worked in black thread, but any colour can be used. Interlaced patterns (such as those used in Celtic designs) can look very effective when worked in this stitch.

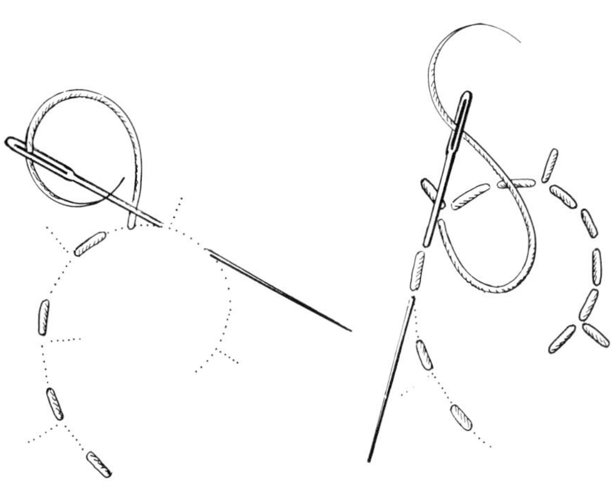

Fig. 67. Holbein or double running stitch, usually worked on an evenweave fabric. The shape to be outlined is first worked in running stitch. On the return journey the spaces are filled in, creating a continuous line

Assissi work

Assissi embroidery combines double running stitch and cross stitch. The designs, often animals, are outlined in double running stitch and then left unworked, while the background is covered in cross stitch. Traditional colours are red for the cross stitch and black for Holbein stitch.

Blackwork

Blackwork is basically Holbein, or double running stitch, used to build up various geometric patterns. It first appeared in this country in the sixteenth century, and is said to have been introduced by Katherine of Aragon, although there is

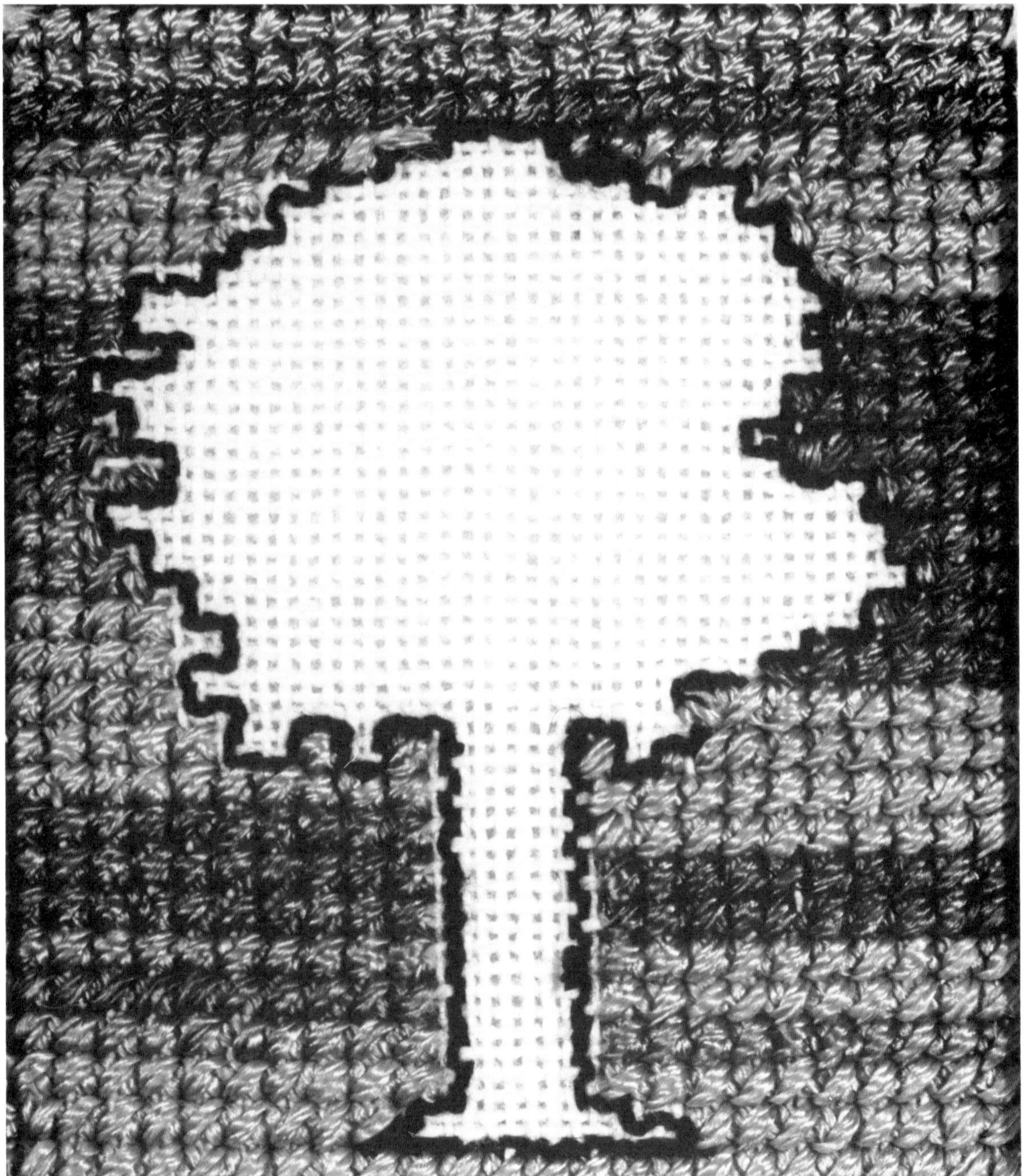

Fig. 68. Assissi work. The background stitches have been worked in a multi-coloured thread to produce tonal interest (Frances Roche)

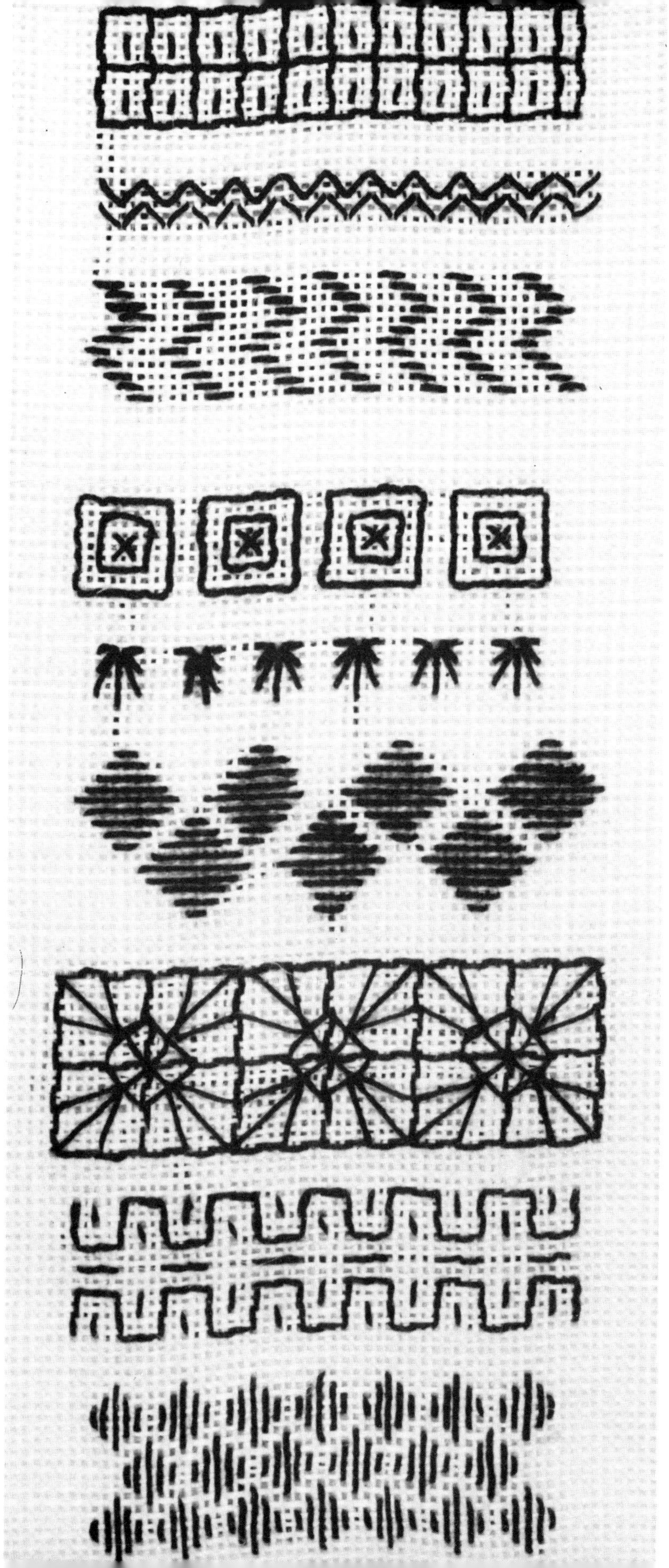

Fig. 69. Sampler of blackwork patterns (Barbara Mellor)

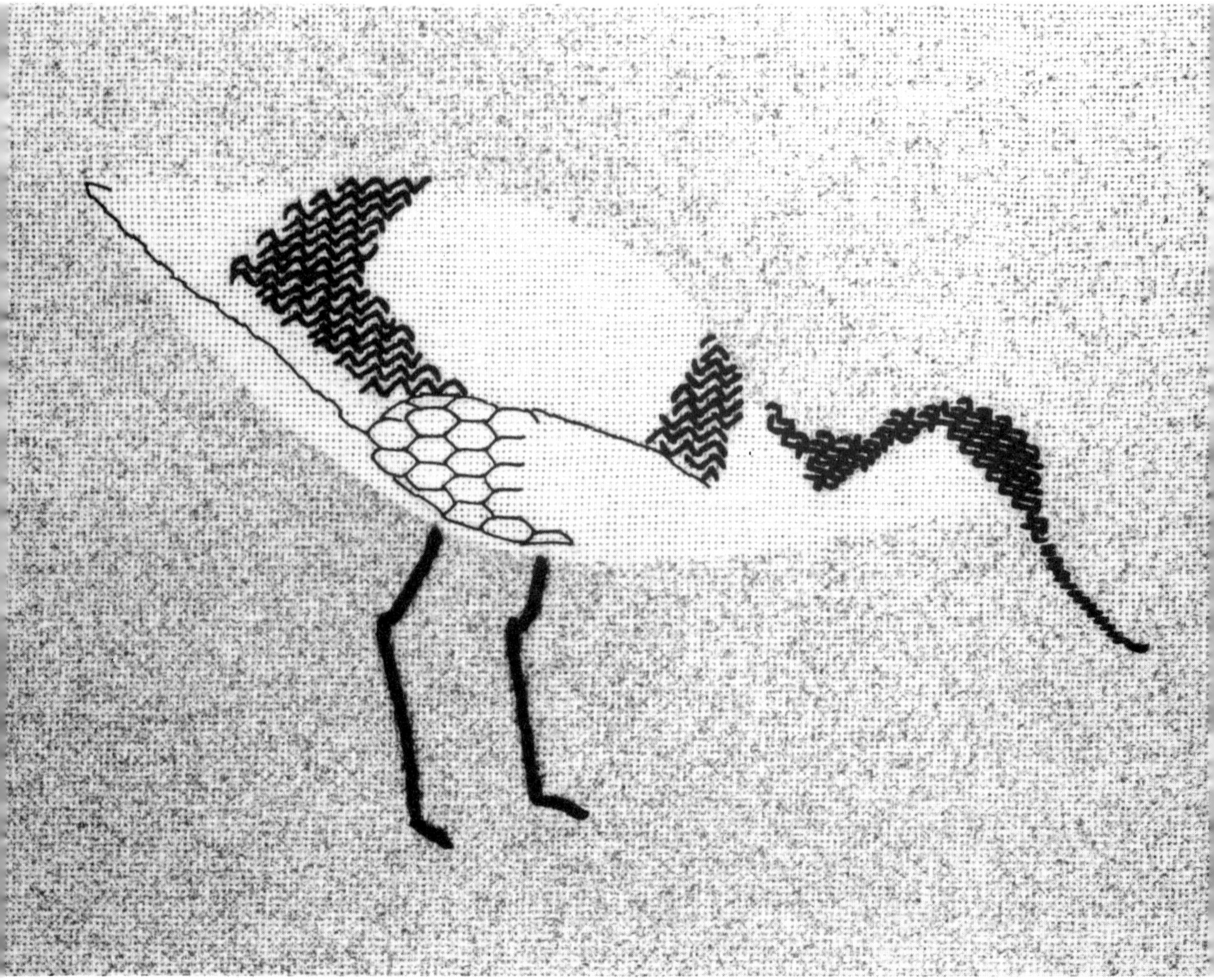

Fig. 70. The shape of the avocet has been cut out in paper and pinned to the linen, before being sprayed with black paint. A minimum of stitchery was needed to embroider the bird (Nancy Woodman)

no firm evidence of this. It was certainly a very popular form of costume embroidery at that time, as can be seen from the many portraits of the Tudor kings and queens and their courtiers. It was used to decorate bed hangings and pillows as well as garments. The designs often consisted of formal flower designs filled in with tiny geometric patterns.

Is should be worked on an evenweave fabric. It is much more interesting to use a variety of thicknesses of thread, from fine sewing cotton to thick wools. Traditionally, black thread is used. Colour can look very effective, but should be handled carefully as blackwork depends on its tonal effects to build up a design, and this can be lost when using colour.

It is worth working a small sampler of patterns. A few are shown here, but you should experiment with your own. Use a variety of threads and try working the same pattern in thick as well as thin threads. Restrict the numbers of patterns, as it is much more interesting to work a few in interesting ways than many in just one quality of thread.

Black and white newspaper photographs provide a good inspiration for blackwork, as they have good tonal contrasts. Choose a photograph that appeals to you, trace off the main outlines and tack to fabric.

Consider using fabric printing as a starting point (a piece of polystyrene dipped in black fabric paint will provide good texture) but do not overload the fabric with paint. Remember that the lightest part of your design will be the white background fabric.

As you stitch, refer constantly to the original photograph. The darkest parts of the photograph will be the most densely stitched parts of the embroidery; this can be built up either by using a heavily stitched pattern or by using a thick thread. For lighter areas, the same patterns could be worked using a finer thread. In fact, the whole design could be executed in one pattern. Do not be afraid to leave some areas unworked, or to trail off the designs to achieve the desired effect. A small touch of gold thread can be added to highlight the work, but be careful not to put in too much. Surface stitches can also be added if required–for instance, small areas of seeding, or use stem or other linear stitches for curved lines.

Fig. 71. Geese embroidered in a variety of blackwork patterns (Diana Mitchell)

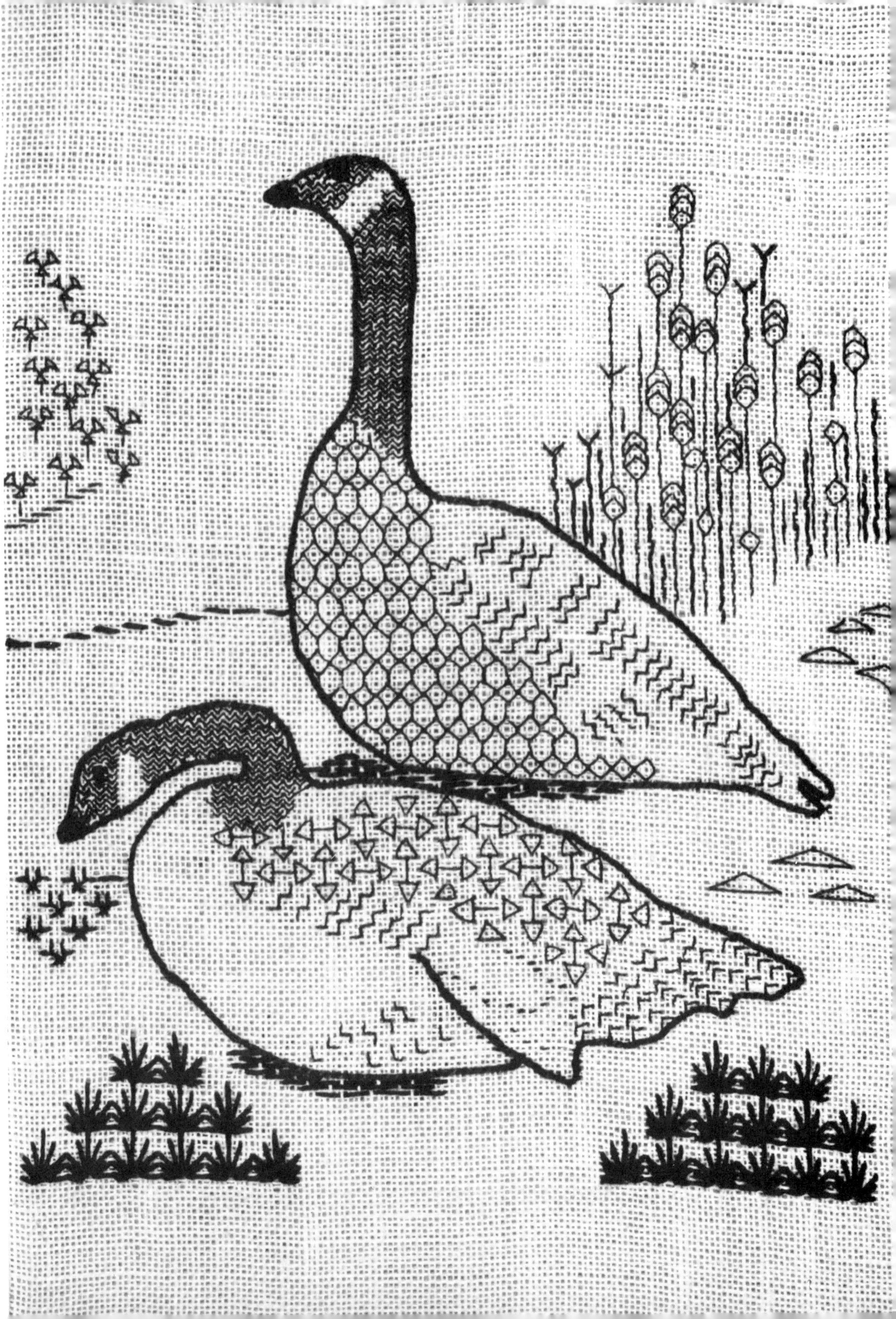

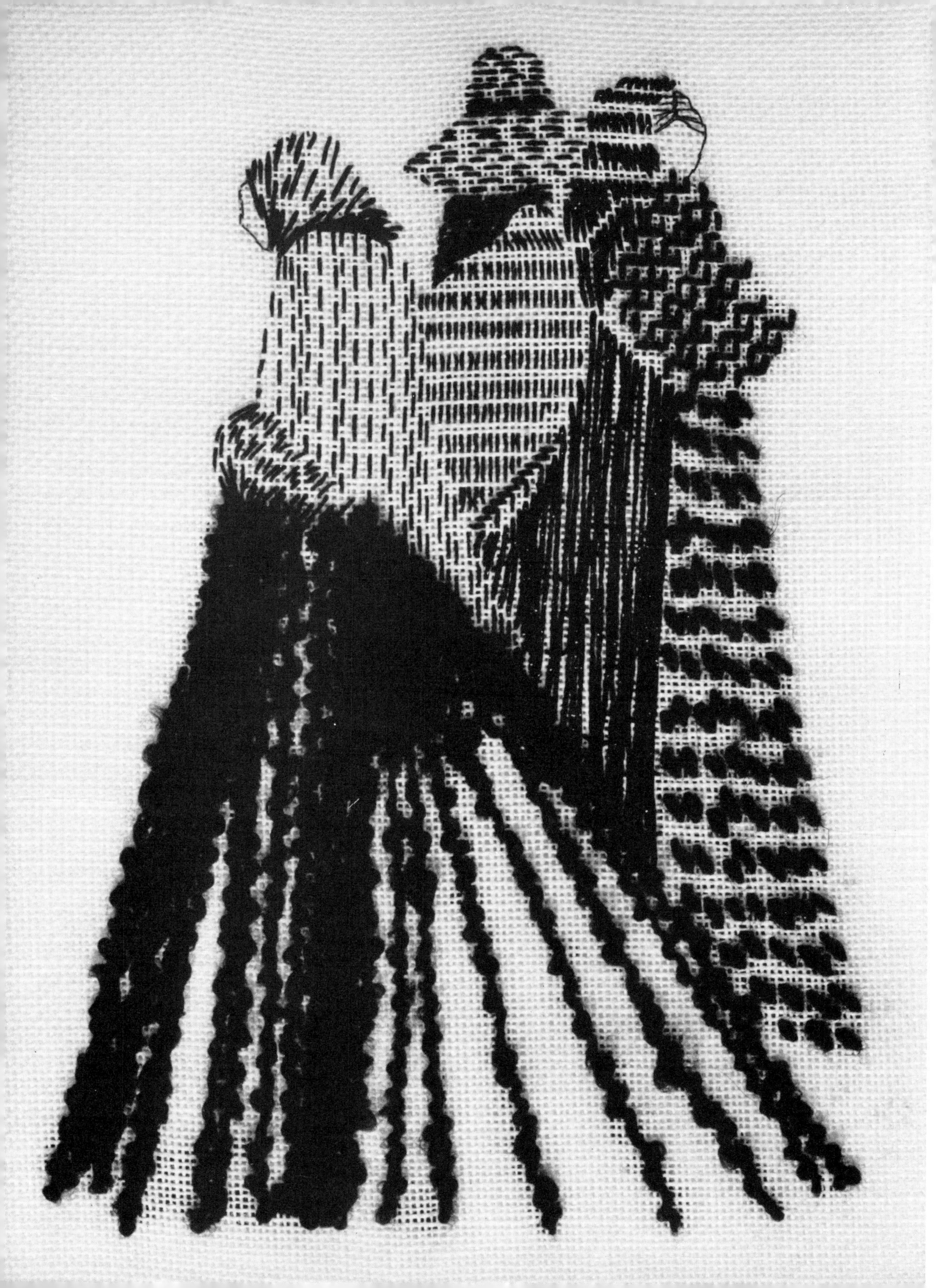

Eight

Finishing off

The construction, and finish, of a piece of embroidery can sometimes take just as long and require as much thought as the embroidery itself. This chapter gives instructions for simple construction methods and finishings, as well as for mounting and framing work.

Stretching

Most embroideries, especially if they have been worked without a frame, will require damp stretching. To do this, cover a board with two or three layers of absorbent paper (blotting paper is suitable). Dampen the paper by spraying with cold, clean water. Plastic spray bottles can be purchased very cheaply in garden centres. Lay the embroidery face up on the paper, and carefully pin in place all round the edges. Use drawing pins for this; keep the fabric as taut as possible and the grain straight. Spray the embroidery until it is quite damp, and leave to dry before removing the drawing pins. When stretching canvas embroidery, particular care should be taken to ensure that the threads of the canvas are returned to the straight grain. If a lot of diagonal stitches are used, the canvas can become very distorted, and may need to be stretched more than once before it is returned to its original shape.

Fig. 72. *Spanish Ladies* in blackwork, using different thicknesses of thread. The skirt of one of the ladies is made up of couched textured wool (Barbara Mellor)

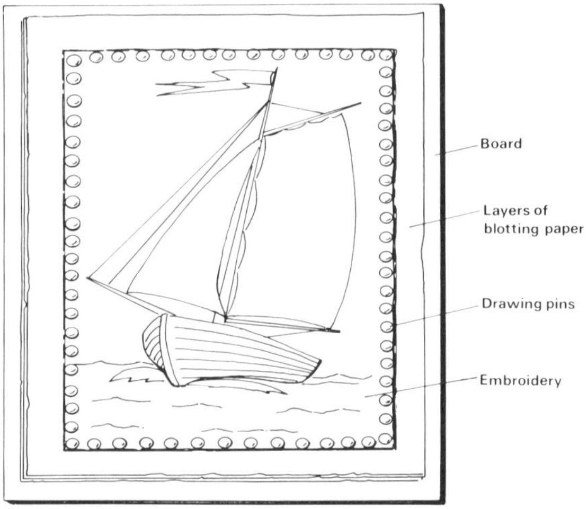

Fig. 73. Re-shaping the finished embroidery. The work should be carefully pinned into its correct shape before being dampened and left to dry

Mounting and framing

Panels should be mounted on a piece of thin wood or very tough card. Establish the exact size required and make sure that the board is accurately cut to these measurements. It is helpful to tack the finished size around the edge of the

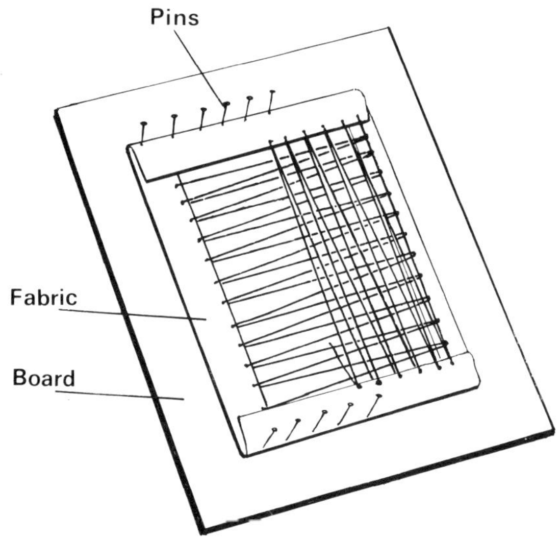

Fig. 74. If it is to be used as a panel to be hung on a wall, the finished embroidery is laced over a piece of mounting card

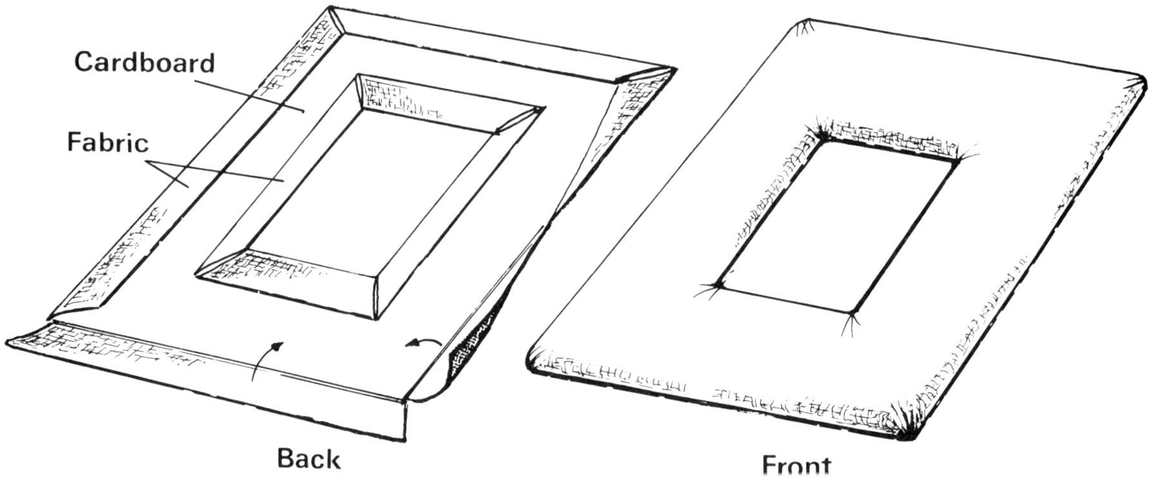

Fig. 75. A fabric-covered mount can be used effectively to frame a piece of embroidery. The fabric may be in a matching or contrasting colour, and sometimes the embroidery is continued across the mount

embroidery before starting. Lay the embroidery face down on a clean, flat surface and place the board in position. Use a strong thread, such as linen or fine string. With a long length of thread, lace opposite sides together, beginning at the centre and working out to the edges. Carefully fold in the corners so that they are hidden on the wrong side. Remember to fasten off securely. To neaten the back of the embroidery, cut a piece of fabric such as calico, turn in the edges and hem stitch into place. A length of cord can be sewn in place to hang the embroidery on the wall.

Fabric frames

If a frame is required, it is possible to purchase one ready made. Card mounts can also be bought in a range of colours. It is, however, a relatively simple matter to make a fabric mount to enhance the embroidery.

The embroidery should first be mounted over a larger piece of board to allow for the frame. Cut a second board the same size, but with a 'window' cut out for the embroidery.

Cut the fabric for the frame, remembering to allow enough extra for turnings. Mark the window measurement on the fabric and cut away, leaving enough fabric for turnings.

Place the fabric right side down on a flat surface with the frame on top. Snip carefully into the corners of the 'window' fabric, and glue in place on the wrong side of the board. A PVA type of adhesive should be used for this. When dry, the outer edges of the frame can be turned under and stitched or glued in place.

Quilts, cushions, etc.

The simplest, most effective way of finishing off quilts or quilted hangings is with a matching strip of fabric. On the grain of the fabric, cut strips about 1½ inches (4 cm) wide. It may be neccessary to join several strips together to achieve the correct length. Neaten all the edges of the quilt or hanging, cutting away surplus wadding. Lay the strip of fabric, right sides together, on the quilt and pin in place. Machine through all the layers ¼ inch (1 cm) from the edge. Turn the strip to the wrong side, turn under the raw edge and hem neatly in place. For hanging purposes, a length of fabric, doubled to about 2 inches (5–6 cm) can be sewn on the reverse of the quilt, just inside the top edge. A piece of dowelling can be slotted through the sleeve.

Continuous bias strip

If the quilt has a curved edge, a bias strip should be used to bind it. It is quite easy to cut a continuous strip.

Cut a square of fabric and fold it half diagonally. Cut the fabric along this line.

Machine the two resulting triangles together, along two short straight edges. Press the seam open. The fabric should now resemble a parallelogram, with the long edges top and bottom, rather than a square. Using a pencil and ruler, mark the correct width strips on the fabric.

On the wrong side, bring the two bias edges together and pin and machine the seam, remembering to drop down one bias strip at top and bottom. Begin cutting on the marked lines at one end. As you cut, a continuous strip of fabric will be formed.

Piped edge

Cord for piping can be purchased in different sizes and types of material. Check that it is preshrunk. If not, place it in a pan of boiling water and let it simmer for several minutes. Allow to dry before using. The fabric should always be cut on the bias. The width required will depend on the thickness of the cord used, but it should be wide enough to surround the cord and give a good seam allowance.

Place the cord in the centre of the wrong side of the bias strip. Fold the strip in half and tack in place. Stitch down the strip as close as possible to the piping cord.

To use as an edging, sandwich the cord between the right side of the fabric and the lining, with all the raw edges meeting. Pin and tack in place and then carefully machine as close as possible to the piping. Neaten off and turn to the right side. When turning a corner, pin the piping carefully into place; do not pull it or the corners will not remain square and it will spoil the look of the finished cushion.

To join lengths of piping cord, unpick the fabric strip for ¾ or 1 inch (2 or 3 cm) on each side. Trim the cord so that there is an overlap of ¾ or 1 inch (2 or 3 cm). Unravel the cords and trim the pieces to different lengths. Twist the remaining pieces together (they can be secured with sewing cotton) and recover with fabric.

Purchased or hand-made cords can also be used to trim cushions and bags.

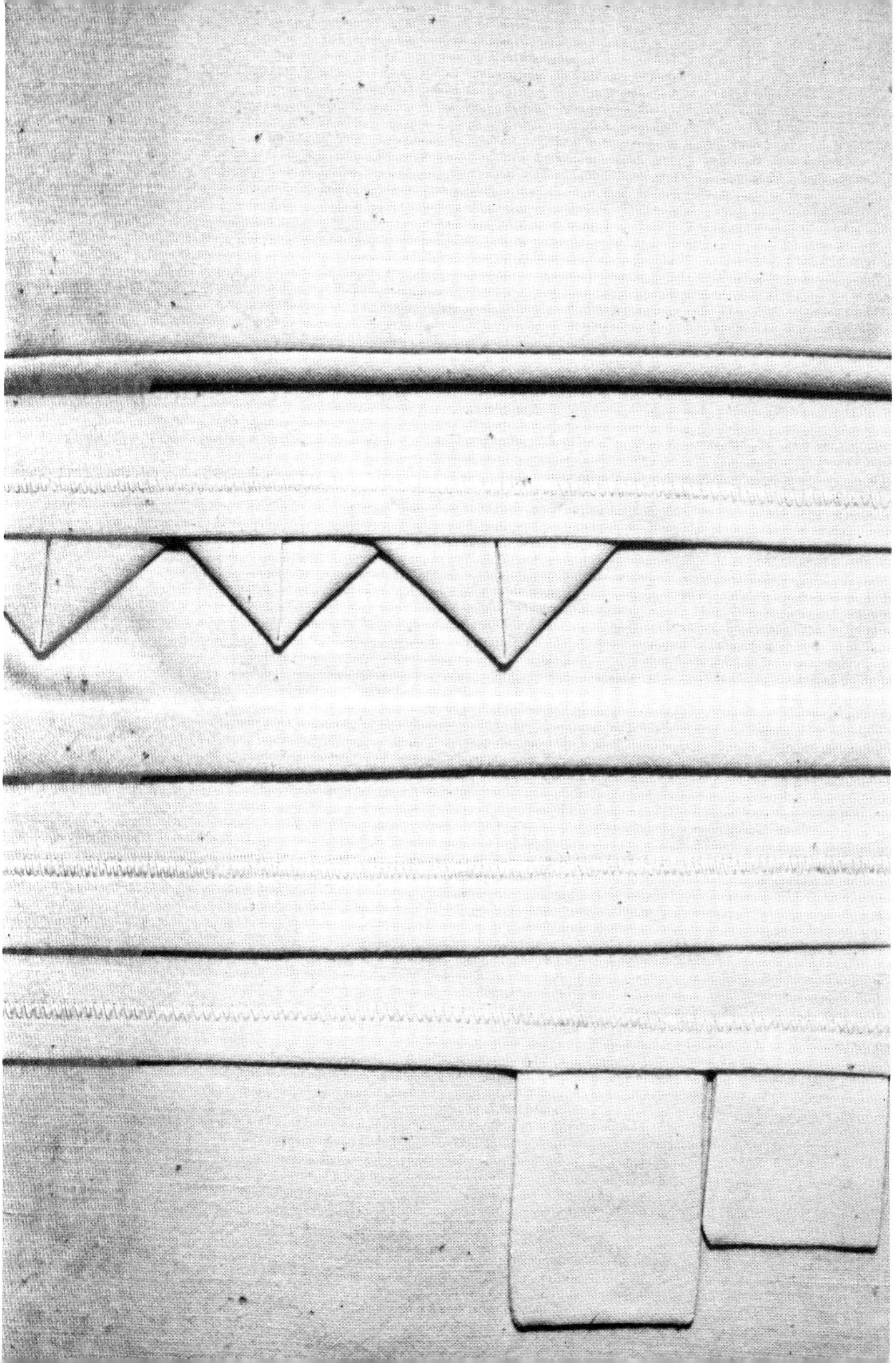

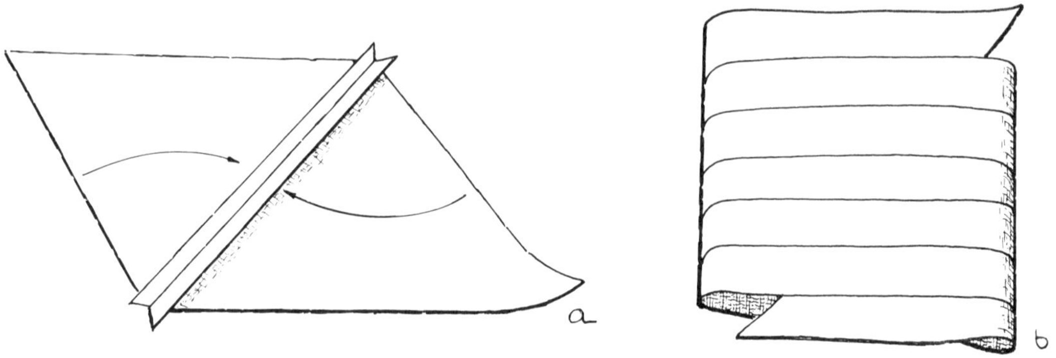

Hand-made cords

Simple cords can be made with great effect; they will be much cheaper than purchased cords and the colour can be matched exactly to the embroidery.

Twisted cord is the simplest of all to do. Two people will be needed to do this. Cut lengths of thread approximately three times the required length. Knot the ends into a loop and insert a pencil in either end, so that it is quite taut. Keep the threads taut and twist the pencils in opposite directions, until the threads twist up on themselves. Remove the pencils and fold the cord in half; it will twist itself together.

Machine-made cords can be done very quickly with a sewing machine that has a swing needle stitch. Use a firm, medium thickness string (macrame twine is ideal) Set the machine to its widest swing, and a close stitch. Place the string under the foot and stitch down the length. String can also be wrapped by hand, but this is a much more time-consuming business.

Fig. 76. Some methods of finishing the edges of embroideries. From top: a) piped edge b) fabric turned under and machined in place with the zigzag stitch (The decorative triangles are formed from a square of fabric, folded in half and then the corners folded down to form a triangle) c) bias strip round edge d) machine zig-zag finish (The tabs are strips of folded fabric, sewn up the sides and then turned to the right side)

Fig. 77. Continuous bias strip. a) A square of fabric is cut on the diagonal and two straight edges machined together
b) After the strips have been marked on the fabric, it is joined into a tube, remembering to 'drop' the fabric by the width of one strip

Tassels

Tassels can be used to great effect to trim embroidery, whether it is a tiny bag or a large wall hanging. They can be made of any type of thread from fine silk to thick wools, strips of leather and ribbons. They can be quite simple or have elaborately beaded and embroidered heads.

Cut a piece of card to the required length and wind thread around it. Cut a separate length of thread and slip it through the loops at one end of the card. Fasten together securely. Cut the loops at the other end.

Take a second length of thread and tie the tassel together about 1 inch (2 cm) from the looped end. If required, the head can be covered with detached buttonhole stitch to give added texture. Small beads can also be sewn around the tassel or threaded to the ends of the tassel and tied in place. The head of the tassel can be completely wrapped with thread.

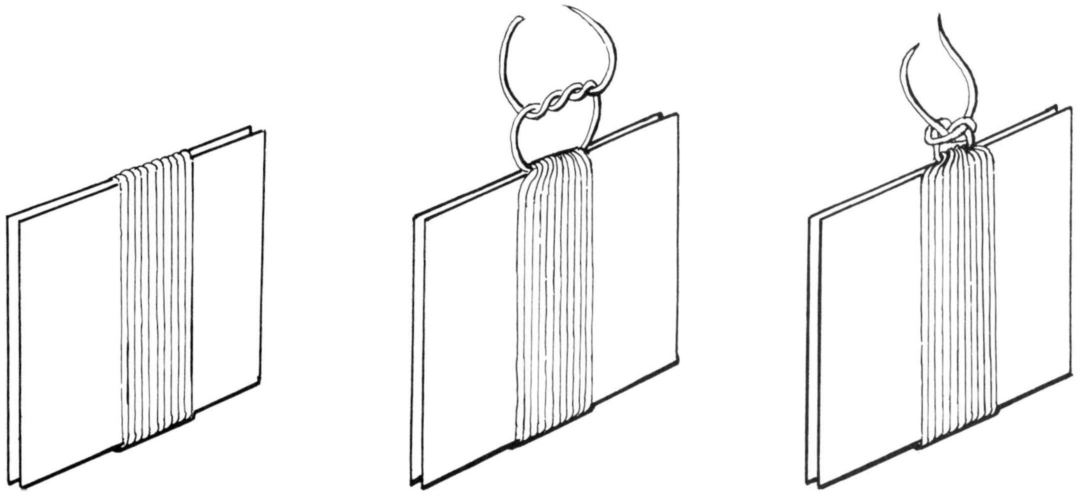

Buttons

It is possible nowadays to buy many interesting and beautiful buttons to add to your embroidery. Fabric buttons can be made over purchased moulds.

Dorset wheel buttons are quite simple to make and can be made in a thread to match the embroidery.

Use a metal or plastic curtain ring and cover with buttonhole stitch. Twist the looped edges to the inside (called 'slicking'). Take threads across the ring to form first an upright cross and then a diagonal cross. Secure the threads in the centre with a small cross. Back stitch around each spoke in turn until the button is completed.

Fig. 78. Tassels. Wind thread around a piece of card; slip a length of thread around the loops and fasten securely; cut the loops at one end of the card

Fig. 79. Tassels and cords. From left: a) large tassel made of silk threads attached to a machine-made cord b) hand-twisted cord c) decorative tassel using fine silk threads and hand-made beads d) Dorset button (beads made by Muriel Best)

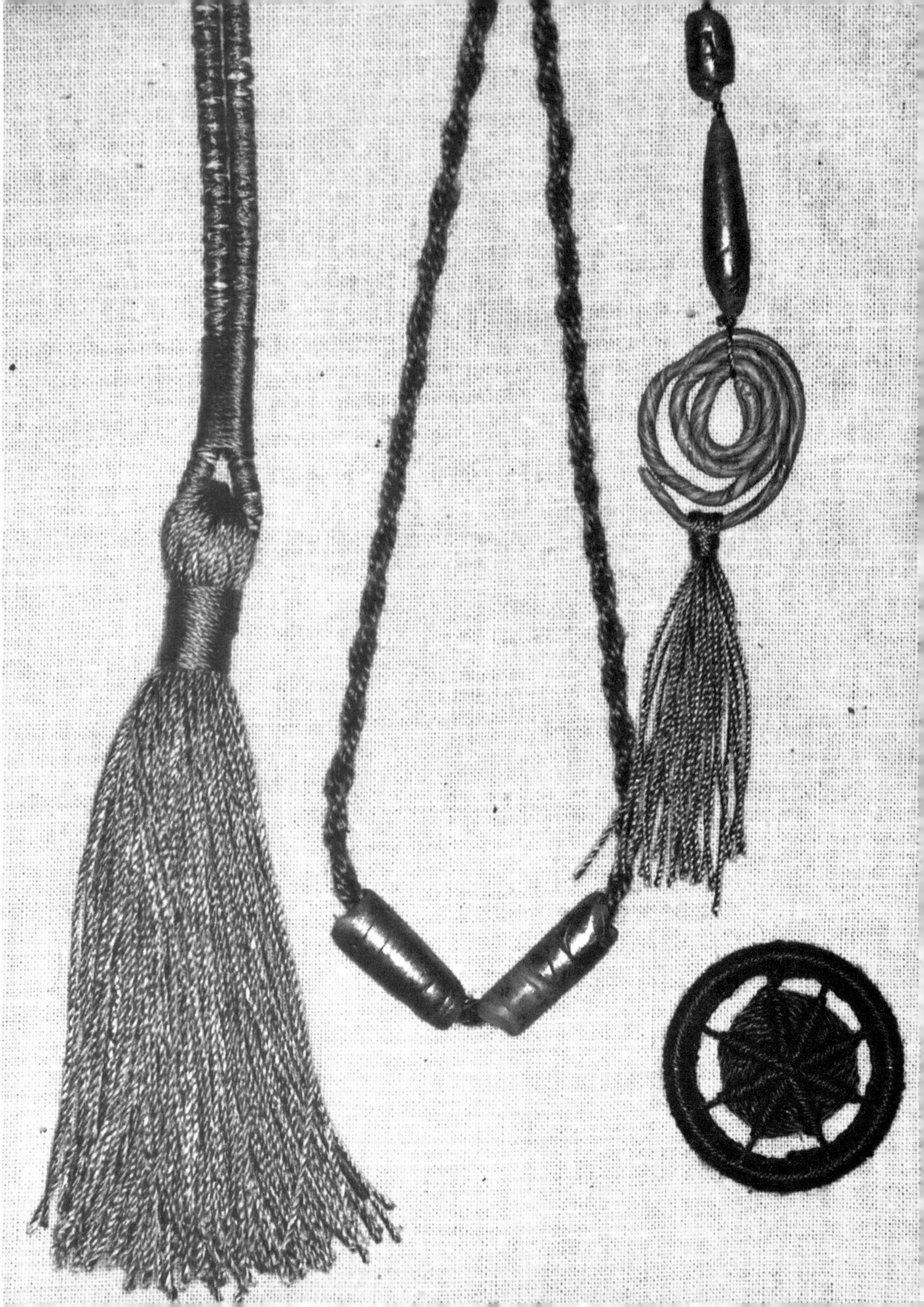

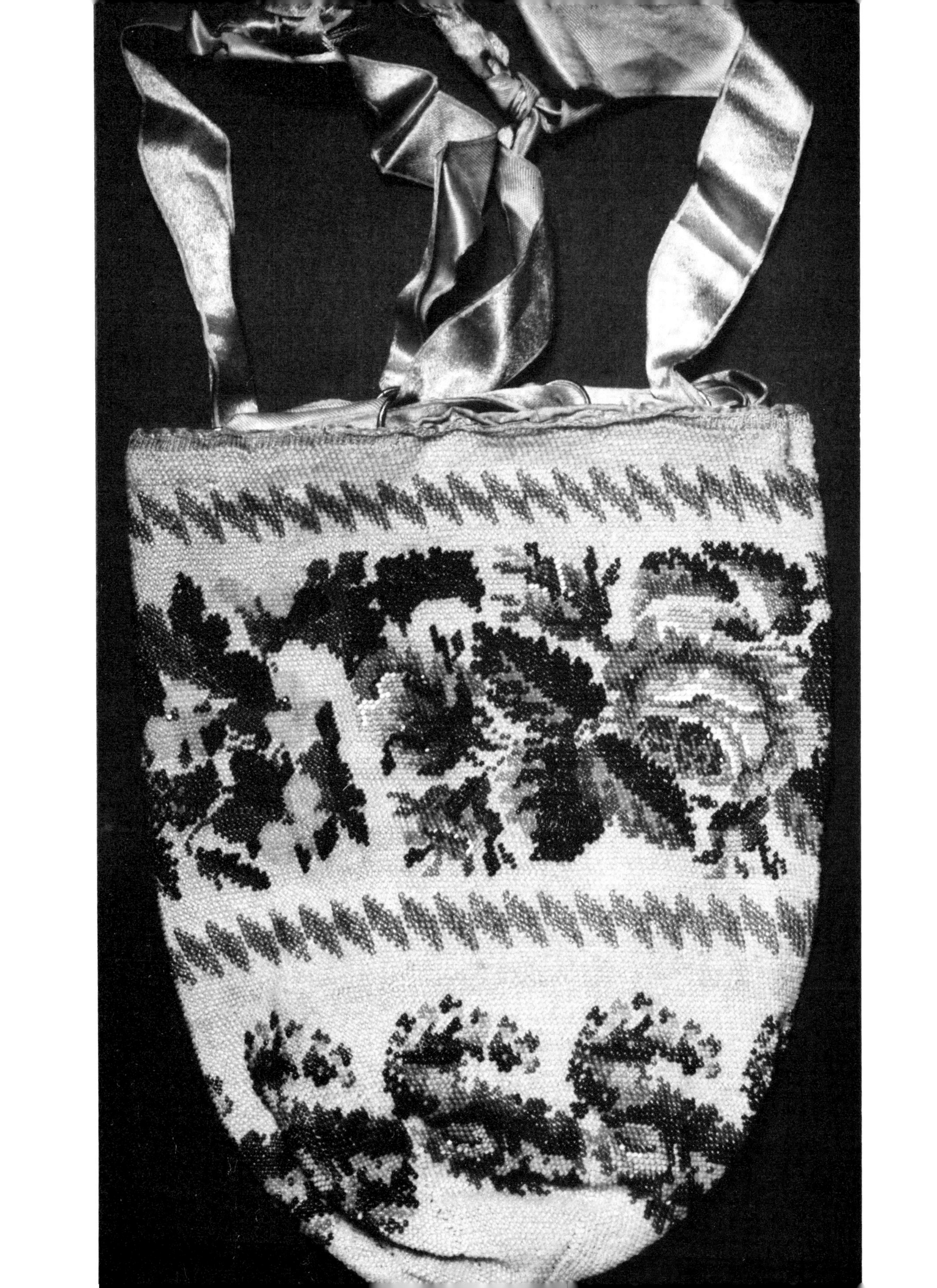

Further reading

Jan Messent, *The Embroiderer's Workbook*, B. T. Batsford

Eiran Short, *Introducing Quilting*, B. T. Batsford

Diana Springall, *Canvas Embroidery*, B. T. Batsford

Margaret Pascoe, *Blackwork*, B. T. Batsford

Mary Thomas, *Dictionary of Stitches*, Hodder & Stoughton

Barbara Snook, *Embroidery Stitches*, Dryad Press

Constance Howard, *Embroidery and Colour*, B. T. Batsford

Brenda Marchbank, *Durham Quilting*, Dryad Press

Dilys Fronks, *Appliquéd Patchwork*, Dryad Press

Margaret Ohms, *Ethnic Embroidery*, Dryad Press

Embroidery, the quarterly magazine of the Embroiderers' Guild

Fig. 80. (overleaf) Small nineteenth-century purse, entirely covered in minute beads forming an intricate floral pattern. The beads are worked on a knitted base. Pink satin ribbon has been threaded through rings sewn at the opening

Suppliers

Barnyarns
Old Pitts Farm
Langrish
Petersfield
Hants GU23 1RQ
Suppliers of a wide range of embroidery threads and materials

Mulberry Silks
Unit 12a
Worcester Road Industrial Estate
Chipping Norton
Oxon OX7 5XW
Silk embroidery threads in a vast range of colours

Mace & Nairn
89 Crane Street
Salisbury
Wilts
Suppliers of threads, linens, canvas, etc.

Borovicks
16 Berwick Street
London W1
Stocks unusual fabrics, including lurex and transparent fabrics

George Weil & Sons Ltd
63–65 Riding House Street
London W1P 7PP
Silk and cotton fabrics, fabric paints and dyes

Whaleys (Bradford) Ltd
Harris Court
Great Horton
Bradford
W. Yorks BD7 4EQ
Enormous range of fabrics including calico, silk, etc.

The Embroiderers' Guild
Apartment 41
Hampton Court Palace
Easy Molesey
Surrey, KT8 9AU
(Publishers of Embroidery magazine)

Index

Batsford Embroidery Titles

Batsford Embroidery Titles

Machine Embroidery
Stitch Techniques
Valerie Campbell-Harding and Pamela Watts
Essential reading for embroiderers wishing to develop and extend their skills and their enjoyment of the sewing machine.
102 illustrations 144 pages 0 7134 5797 X hardback

Kathleen Whyte Embroiderer
Liz Arthur
An entertaining biography and appreciation of the work of Scotland's leading embroiderer.
132 illustrations 144 pages 0 7134 5578 0 hardback

Design Sources for Embroidery
Muriel Best and Vicky Lugg
'This book is a source of inspiration for embroidery, design and textile work.' *Art & Craft*
223 illustrations 168 pages 0 7134 5573 X hardback

Assisi Embroidery
Old Italian Cross-stitch Designs
Eva Maria Leszner
'This book has very clear descriptions of working methods and designs. A delightful book with plenty of information on old Italian cross-stitch.' *West County Embroiderers*
95 illustrations 96 pages 0 7134 5595 0 hardback

The Embroiderer's Workbook
Jan Messent
'. . . contains a wealth of ideas to work through, which as well as being instructive, would provide endless fun.' *West Country Embroiderers*
105 illustrations 96 pages 0 7134 5709 0 hardback

Drawing and Design for Embroidery
A Course for the Fearful
Richard Box
'Newcomers to needlework and experienced embroiderers will both benefit from Richard Box's suggestions.' *Pins & Needles*
120 illustrations 152 pages 0 7134 5574 0 hardback

Stumpwork
Historical and Contemporary Raised Embroidery
Muriel Best
'The methods and stitches can be used in so many ways, which makes it a very useful and informative book to possess.' *West Country Embroiderers*
148 illustrations 128 pages 0 7134 5572 1 hardback

Landscape in Embroidery
Verina Warren
'. . . stimulating and practical . . . The book is a mine of excellent advice and good value for money.' *Embroidery*
202 illustrations 152 pages 0 7134 4567 X hardback

FROM THE BLUE EMBROIDERY PAPERBACK SERIES:

Ecclesiastical Embroidery
Beryl Dean
'For all embroideresses, both expert and amateur, interested in Ecclesiastical embroidery, this book will be a sheer delight.' *Church of England Newspaper*
190 illustrations 252 pages 0 7134 6252 3

Design for Embroidery from Traditional English Sources
Constance Howard
This fully illustrated account of the development of English embroidery shows how old designs can be made the stimulating basis for present-day application.
284 illustrations 204 pages 0 7134 6299 X

Dictionary of Canvas Work Stitches
Mary Rhodes
With descriptions of over 250 stitches this work of reference, by one of the best known canvas work embroiderers, will be of the utmost value.
504 illustrations 240 pages 0 7134 3302 7

Write to us for a complete list of all Batsford embroidery titles at:
B.T. Batsford Ltd, Fitzhardinge Street, London W1H 0AH